FaBULOUS
FeLT

First published in Great Britain 2016

Search Press Limited
Wellwood, North Farm Road,
Tunbridge Wells, Kent TN2 3DR

Photographs by Paul Bricknell

ISBN: 978-1-78221-193-8

Suppliers
For details of suppliers, please visit the
Search Press website: www.searchpress.com

Printed in China

Acknowledgements

This book is dedicated to my late mother who gave me the love of crafts and always
encouraged me to pursue my dream.

I would also like to thank my family, including my three beautiful children for their enthusiasm
about this book and my friends for their cheerful support: Emma, Oonagh and Olivia.

Last but not least, a very big thank you to the Search Press team who have been fabulous,
especially Daniel Conway for his patience and guidance.

FABULOUS FELT

30 easy-to-sew accessories and decorations

Corinne Lapierre

SEARCH PRESS

Contents

Introduction

Ever since I was a little girl growing up with a very creative mother, I have always had a passion for crafts.

My attraction to fabric and sewing is probably what led to me become a fashion designer, but it wasn't until I studied millinery that I discovered felt and knew that I had found my real passion. Since then, I have spent years studying and teaching different techniques of working with felt and I still remain fascinated by the many beautiful qualities of this medium.

I now have my own brand of craft kits in which felt has taken centre stage. Even now, I get a buzz when I look at the different coloured rolls neatly stacked on my shelves!

Felt is one of the most ancient textiles known to man and is used all over the world. The legend goes that shepherds used wool to cushion their feet in their clogs and that the movement, heat and sweat matted it into felt. Making felt really is this simple and its properties make it a very versatile material: it is easy to cut, does not fray and can be stitched easily. It can also be steamed, shaped, glued and layered.

The quality and colours of the felt you buy will really show in your projects so, if possible, I would advise you to use wool felt or a good-quality wool mix.

I hope to share my passion for felt with this collection of thirty felt accessories and decorations. Some projects are quick and easy and others will require more time and patience. All projects are sewn by hand so you don't need to set anything up and you can easily take them with you. Whether you are a complete beginner or a more advanced crafter, I hope you will find plenty of inspiration.

The important thing is that you enjoy making, stitching and mixing colours and you should be very proud of your finished items.

Happy sewing!

Corinne

Materials & equipment

Felt

Throughout this book I have used a wool/viscose blend of felt. It is a more affordable alternative to pure wool while keeping all its luxurious qualities of softness and easy handling. Like pure wool, a wool-mix felt can be gently washed by hand in cold water.

I would really recommend you do not use 100% acrylic felt as the feel of it is very different and it will not be as easy to sew. Sometimes it can be a little thin and see-through too. If you cannot find a good-quality felt on the high street, there are a growing number of online outlets from which you can order felt in beautiful shades and various sizes.

Equipment

The equipment is fairly basic and standard to most sewing kits. You will need some sharp fabric scissors, small pointed embroidery scissors, pins and embroidery needles. You will also be required to use some pencils, pens to transfer the templates and some paper scissors. Fabric pens can be used, although they are optional.

For some projects you will need some double-sided fusible webbing material to stick two pieces of felt together and I also like to have plain tissue paper handy to transfer embroidery patterns (see page 11).

Other materials

To complete all the projects, you will also need some toy stuffing, ribbons, embroidery thread in various colours and dried lavender flowers. A few beads, sequins or pretty buttons always add a personal touch too.

Opposite
Clockwise from top left:
sheets of double-sided fusible webbing,
toy stuffing, ribbons, dried lavender
flowers, embroidery thread and wool/
viscose blend felt in varying colours.

From left to right:
embroidery scissors,
embroidery needles,
pins and fabric scissors.

Techniques

Transferring templates

1 Cut out your paper template (photocopied or traced from the book) and place on the felt. Hold or pin in place and draw around it with a pencil or pen.

2 Remove the paper template and use your fabric scissors to cut the felt following the line you drew.

3 You can double-check your felt shape against the template for size and accuracy.

TIP: The dotted line on the pattern templates indicates a fabric fold. You must fold your felt and align the fold line against the dotted line before cutting out through both layers. Open out to reveal the complete shape.

Preparing embroidery thread

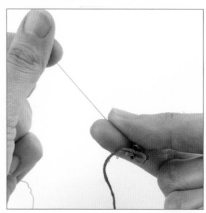

1 From the·skein cut a length of about 60 to 70cm (23½ to 27½in). Holding the thread loosely, take one or two strands at one end.

2 Gently pull the strand(s) from the rest of the length, which will twist into a ball. This will not tangle it; it will go back to normal once you have taken the strand(s) out.

Tissue paper templates

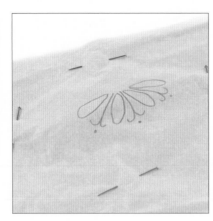

1 Place a piece of plain white tissue paper on the template in the book and carefully trace the embroidery pattern.

2 Pin the tissue paper securely onto the felt you wish to embroider with the traced lines showing on top.

3 Start embroidering as you would normally, but going through the felt and the tissue paper (from the top). Pull the needle through very gently as you might find that it tears the tissue paper a little bit. Do not worry if this happens, just keep stitching.

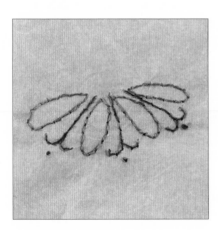

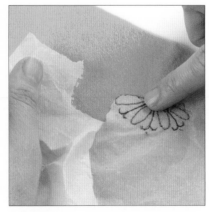

4 When you have finished the embroidery it should look like this, with the stitches showing on top of the tissue paper.

5 Place your work on the table and hold the stitches firmly with your finger while you pull very gently on the tissue paper to remove it. It tends to tear around the stitching. Be very cautious not to disturb the embroidery by pulling too hard. This is why holding the stitches is so important.

Appliqué

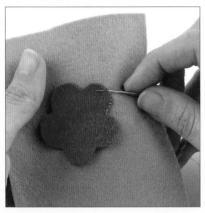

Technique 1

Place the cut-out shape of felt onto the larger piece you want to attach it to. You can hold it or pin it and sew it on with small regular overhand stitches. If you want the appearance to be very discreet, use thread of a similar colour to the felt.

Technique 2

Another technique consists of layering shapes of felt and sewing them in place with bold embroidery stitches in a contrasting colour. The stitches become part of the design, but also serve the purpose of attaching the pieces.

Technique 3

1 Use double-sided fusible webbing material. Simply place the glue side onto the felt and set your iron to the manufacturer's recommended temperature. Iron for a few minutes on the paper side, until the glue has melted.

2 Once the felt and paper have cooled down, transfer the shape you wish to make from the template onto the paper and cut with your fabric scissors.

3 Peel off the paper from the felt. You should now be able to see a shiny residue on the felt which is the glue.

4 Position your felt shape onto the base you wish to attach it to, glue side down. Iron on a warm setting for a few minutes. This will make the glue melt and bond the two layers of felt together. You can leave it as it is or add embroidery.

Attaching a hanging loop

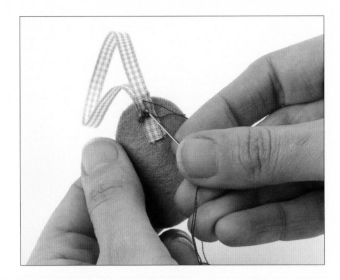

1 Fold a piece of ribbon in half to form a loop. Place the ends together on the wrong side of the back piece of your project. Sew a couple of times through the ribbon and the felt with small straight stitches to hold it in place.

2 Place the front piece of the project on top and stitch through both layers of felt and the ribbon to hold it securely in place. Use pins to secure the layers if needed. Carry on stitching around the edges with the recommended stitch (usually blanket stitch).

Stuffing a project

3 When you have sewn about three-quarters of the way round your piece, do not cut the thread, but take small amounts of toy stuffing and push them inside the gap. Carry on stitching to close the gap and end the sewing where you started.

4 If you are filling your project with lavender, use the same technique as for toy stuffing. I would always advise putting a small amount of toy stuffing at the bottom of the project to seal the seam. Add the lavender in small pinches. If you do this over a bowl or tray, you can collect what falls out. Add a tiny bit of toy stuffing to finish, then carry on stitching to close the gap completely.

Embroidery stitches

M ost of the projects in this book use standard, very well-known embroidery stitches. If you haven't done any embroidery or hand sewing before, you might want to practise them on a scrap of felt. The most useful ones to remember are backstitch and blanket stitch.

In almost every one of my projects, I like to use the embroidery and the sewing as a part of the design. I suggest being bold and using contrasting colours. Don't worry if your stitches are not regular, as it all adds a very personal 'handmade' feel – I see the stitching almost as a drawing process.

For all your embroidery, split your thread and use only one, two or three strands (see page 10). Make a knot at the end of the thread and always start from the wrong side, hiding the knot. Now bring the needle through to the right side.

Running stitch

1 Running stitch is extremely simple with the needle going in and out of the fabric at regular intervals to create a line of evenly spaced stitches.

Backstitch

In hand sewing, this stitch is extremely useful for creating straight or curved lines. The trick is to keep the stitches very regular in length and to avoid any gaps.

 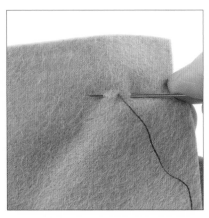 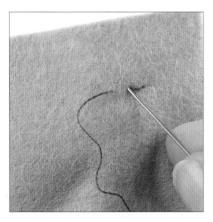

1 After bringing the needle and thread through from the wrong side, push the needle back into the fabric a small space to the right, creating a backstitch.

2 Bring the needle back through a small space to the left, from where you first started. Pull the needle and thread though gently.

3 Pass the needle back to the right to exactly the same spot you had first come out. This will ensure there is no gap in the line of stitching. Continue in this manner, always going back to the previous stitch.

French knot

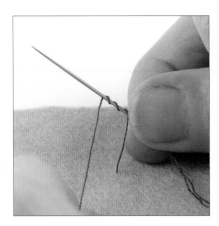 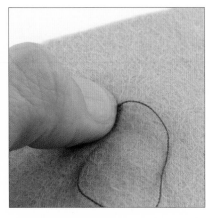 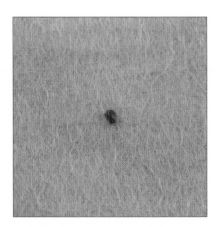

1 With your needle brought out at the front of the fabric, hold it, pointed side upward, take the thread quite close to where it comes out of the felt and twist it round the needle two or three times. Hold the loose end of the thread taut to keep the loops nice and tight on the needle.

2 Still holding onto the end of the thread, push your needle through the felt very close to where it came out (about 2mm/ $^1/_{16}$ in). When the needle is almost through, let go of the thread and use your thumbnail to hold the loops of thread in place while you very gently pull the rest of the needle and thread though.

3 The result is a lovely 3D knot which is perfect to use as eyes for small creatures or to add a dotty effect to your projects.

Blanket stitch (for appliqué)

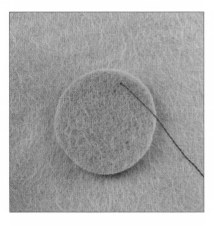

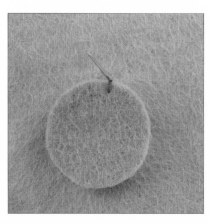

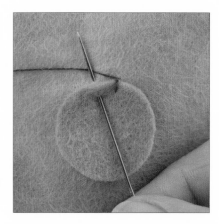

1 Place the shape you wish to use as a felt appliqué onto the larger piece of felt. Hold or pin in place and bring your needle up to the front through both pieces of felt.

2 Push the needle through the back of the project right on the edge of the appliqué shape so that it only goes through one layer of felt (blue) and creates a small straight stitch.

3 Bring the needle back through to the front close to where it just went in and catch the thread of that first stitch on the top edge. Pulling your thread to the left, push the needle through both layers of felt, a small space to the left of the first stitch. Bring it back out through the blue layer on the edge of the green felt.

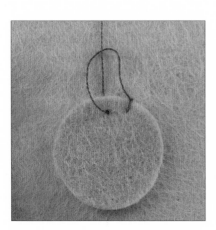

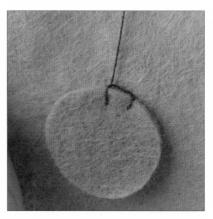

4 Make sure the needle comes out above the thread you have been holding to the left. When you pull through, this will form a small loop being held by the last stitch.

5 Repeat steps 3 to 4, ensuring you keep the spaces and length of stitches regular. Sew all the way round the shape until you reach your first stitch again and bring your needle to the back to end with a secure knot.

Blanket stitch (for finishing edges)

This is a great stitch to use to sew the front and back pieces of a project together.

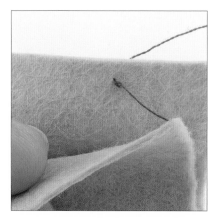

1 Place the knot on the wrong side of the back piece of the project. Bring your needle through to the back.

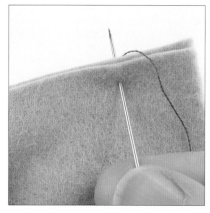

2 Place the front piece of the project on top so that the knot is hidden between the two pieces of felt. Push the needle through both layers a few millimetres (about 1/8in) down from the edge of the fabric so that you have formed a small, straight, vertical stitch.

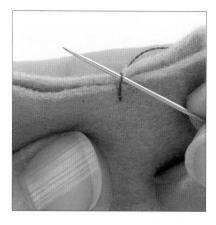

3 Bring your needle through this stitch on the edges of the felt so that it catches the vertical stitch.

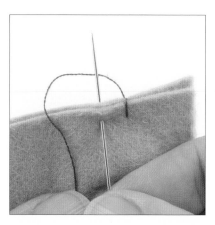

4 With the loose bit of thread going to the left, push the needle through both layers of the fabric a short distance to the left of the first stitch in the same way as your first stitch. Bring it through the loop of thread being formed at the top.

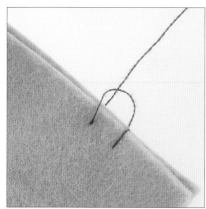

5 Gently pull the needle and thread through the loop so that it holds it in place.

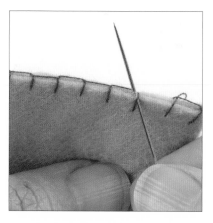

6 Keep repeating steps 4 and 5 to make small regular stitches that hold the loops in place all the way round your project until you reach your first stitch again. End with a knot.

Lazy daisy stitch

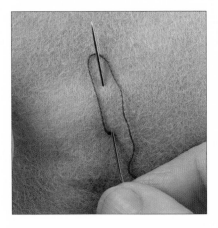 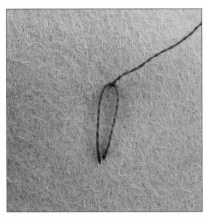 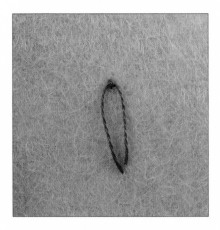

1 With your needle brought through from the back to the front of the fabric, form a petal-shaped loop with the thread and then re-insert the needle back into the fabric very close to where it came out, Bring it out again inside the loop of thread.

2 Very gently pull the needle and thread through as you want to keep the round shape of the petal. If you pull too hard, you might lose the roundness of it.

3 Push your needle back into the felt on the other side of the petal loop so that it forms a tiny little stitch like a bridge holding it in place.

Star stitch

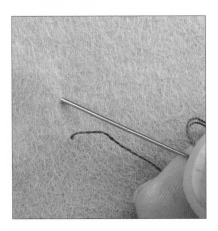 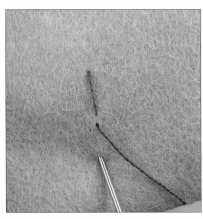 

1 Keep in mind how big you want your star to be and make a small straight stitch which will be almost half the size of the finished star.

2 Leaving a tiny gap, make another small straight stitch in line with the first stitch. This will be the first line of your star.

3 Repeat the stitches to create a + shape and then an X shape emanating from the same central point. You should end up with a star shape as shown.

Mock feather stitch

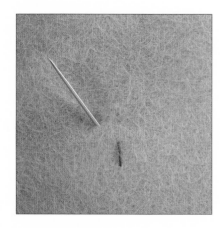

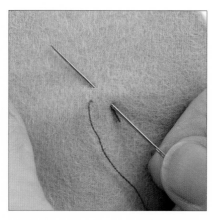

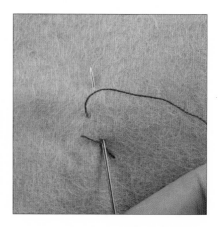

1 First make a small straight stitch which will be the base of the central line and then bring your needle back to the front on the left, slightly above the first stitch. This will create the first little stem off the main line.

2 Bring the needle back into the hole of the top of the first stitch (the central line) and out, following a vertical line to create another small stitch along this central line.

3 With the needle going back to the previous stitch, bring it out again to the right, slightly above, to create another little stem off the main line but this time on the right.

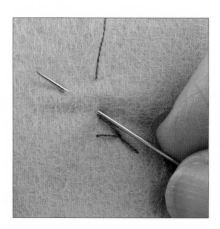

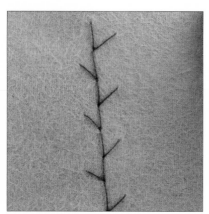

4 Come back to the previous stitch on the central line to create another straight stitch.

5 Keep repeating steps 2 to 4 to create straight stitches as the central line with alternate stems to the right and left so that the final result looks like a branch with little stems on each side.

Summer garden

Try these five simple yet effective projects, including flowers, animals and seaside-themed decorations to bring a little summer sunshine into your home throughout the year. Choose felt in beautiful bright colours or soft pastel shades to give these designs a truly personal touch.

Beach Hut Bunting

Colourful beach huts by the sea are a sight that always delights me. I have drawn them many times because they remind me of holidays and bring a smile to my face. By using soft retro colours, this bunting will bring that seaside feeling to your home with a little vintage touch. The bunting is rather small and looks lovely on a shelf. You could, of course, make it much longer to hang on a wall or make bigger huts by enlarging the pattern. Hang it in your bathroom, kitchen, living room, in a bedroom or even in the garden. You can change the design of each hut as you please, so it's great fun to make.

YOU WILL NEED

- Hut, mini bunting and round window templates (page 126)

MATERIALS (for 4 huts)

- 1 metre (40in) of ribbon

- 4 pieces of felt (approximately 20 x 15cm/ 7¾ x 6in) plus a few scraps of other colours of felt for embellishments (5 x 5cm/ 2 x 2in is enough)

- Contrasting embroidery threads (2 or 3 colours)

TOOLS

- Scissors (paper, fabric and embroidery)

- Pen or pencil

- Embroidery needle

- Pins

1 Cut out the templates and transfer to the felt. Think carefully about how you wish to mix your colours on each hut. For each hut you will need two hut pieces, one roof and a rectangle of 2 x 3cm (¾ x 1¼in) for the door. To decorate the huts you can choose to cut one round window, add colourful planks by cutting strips of 5 x 1cm (2 x ½in) or make mini bunting by cutting five small triangles with the bunting template.

2 For better results, I would advise splitting your thread and using only one or two strands as all the stitches will need to be small and delicate (see page 10). Attach the door using running stitch. You could also try decorating the door with a French knot for a door knob, or perhaps adding a number or a name using backstitch.

3 If you wish to add a window, simply place it in the middle of the roof area and attach with blanket stitch. To add colourful planks on the front façade, place the strips horizontally at regular intervals and stitch in place with running or blanket stitch. If you wish to add some bunting above the door, thread your needle with two or three strands of embroidery thread, stitch through the top corner of the house piece a couple of times (this will be covered by the roof), sew through the top of the five little triangles and end by stitching through the opposite top corner of the house.

4 Place the roof piece on top of the hut and sew with running stitch close to the lower edge of the roof. If you added bunting, the roof piece should cover the ends to make it look neat.

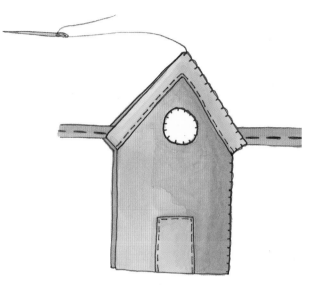

5 When you have decorated the front of all four huts, lay out the backs on your work surface. Place the ribbon on top, going across the base of the roofs. Leave about 25cm (10in) at each end, and spread out the huts at regular intervals, about 9cm (3½in) apart. Add the decorated front façades on top so that the ribbon is sandwiched between the fronts and backs. Pin to hold in place. Sew each hut all round with blanket stitch, making sure you catch the ribbon when you get to it. If you like, you can decorate your ribbon with simple running stitches in a contrasting thread.

Rose Brooches

Roses are some of my favourite flowers and I always marvel at the fold of the petals. There are so many ways artists and crafters have tried to represent them. These little brooches are really easy and fun to make. I like the fact that they form a perfect little ball and are full of folds. They will look great in bright colours but also in more subtle pastels. Wear two or three together on a coat or hat. You could also make them and glue them on wooden sticks or twigs to keep in a vase.

YOU WILL NEED

- Circle template (page 126)

MATERIALS (per brooch)
- 1 piece of felt at least 16 x 16cm (6¼ x 6¼in)
- Matching sewing thread
- Brooch pin

TOOLS
- Scissors (paper, fabric and embroidery)
- Pen or pencil
- Sewing needle
- Fabric glue (optional)

1 Cut out the template and transfer to the felt, drawing round it with a pencil: you will need sixteen circles per brooch. Cut out each felt circle.

2 Place one felt circle flat on your work surface. This will be the base, which will stay flat. Thread your needle and, taking a matching felt circle, fold it in half then fold one side down about one third and then fold the bottom third in the other direction so it folds underneath forming a pointed cone with an S shaped fold (see illustrations below).

3 Place the pointed end of your cone in the centre of the flat base with the edges aligned. Stitch through the point a couple of times to secure it. Do not cut your thread; but keep it ready for the next cone.

4 Repeat to fold the other circles. Place six folded circles quite tightly together to cover the base, stitching them securely one after the other at the point. Keep the thread uncut. Make another layer with six more circles and another with the remaining three more on top, a bit more spaced out. Bring your needle to the back of the base and finish with a secure knot.

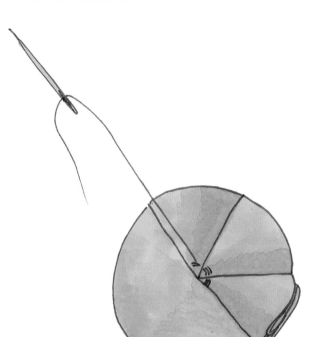

5 Stitch or glue a brooch pin on the back (see the illustration below).

Fluff up the petals to give your flower a nice full and rounded shape.

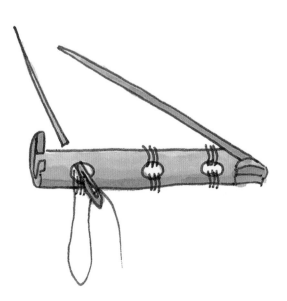

Flower Brooches

These flower brooches are extremely easy to make with minimal sewing. They can be made in minutes using scraps of felt and make lovely gifts, adding a touch of brightness to any outfit. Instead of using felt you could also use some printed cotton fabric for one of the layers.

YOU WILL NEED

- Base and flower template (page 126)

MATERIALS (per brooch)
- 2 pieces of felt at least 10 x 6cm (4 x 2¼in) in contrasting colours
- Double-sided fusible webbing, 10 x 6cm (4 x 2¼in)
- 1 shell button about 1cm (½in) in diameter
- Matching embroidery thread or thick sewing thread
- Brooch pin

TOOLS
- Iron
- Scissors (paper, fabric and embroidery)
- Pen or pencil
- Embroidery needle
- Fabric glue (optional)

1 Following Technique 3 on page 12 for layering fabric with double-sided fusible webbing, attach the two pieces of contrasting coloured felt together. Do not cut the felt at this point, simply iron the fusible material to one piece of felt and wait for it to cool down. Peel off the paper and place the other piece of felt on top; iron for a couple of minutes until it is securely glued together.

2 Cut out the templates and transfer to the double-sided felt, drawing around them with a pencil. You will need one circle and one flower. Cut out the felt. You will find it easier if you use very sharp pointed scissors such as embroidery scissors.

3 Place the flower on top of the circle, showing the contrasting sides. Centre your flower and place the button on top, in the middle. Starting from the back, stitch a few times through all layers to hold everything in place. Finish with a knot at the back.

4 Stitch or glue the brooch pin on the back as with the Rose Brooches (see page 29).

Lavender Sardines

These little sardines make me smile and bring a touch of seaside to my bathroom, and they are also practical with their scented qualities. They are good fun to make and a great project for practising your embroidery. I like to hang two or three together. You could also make them as a gift and present them in a little tin for a touch of humour.

YOU WILL NEED

- Sardine template (page 123)

MATERIALS (per sardine)

- 1 piece of felt at least 10 x 15cm (4 x 6in)
- Contrasting embroidery thread
- 20cm (8in) of thin hemp rope or string
- Loose dried lavender flowers, about 10g (⅓oz)
- A pinch of toy stuffing (optional)

TOOLS

- Scissors (paper, fabric and embroidery)
- Pen or pencil
- Embroidery needle

1 Cut out the template and transfer to the felt. You will need two fish shapes. Cut the felt.

2 Cut a length of thread and split it to use only two or third strands. Start by embroidering the front and back of the sardine. Use a French knot for the eye and single mock feather stitches (see below) to make the scales. Keep them slightly loose to keep the round shape. Alternatively, you can make a zigzag pattern with a simple straight stitch, which is a little bit easier (as shown on the red sardine). Running stitches and French knots can add interesting patterns too. Be as creative as you want with the pattern!

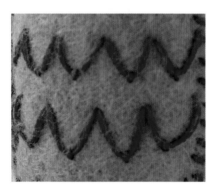

3 When you have embroidered both sides, attach the piece of string, knotted into a loop, into the fish's mouth (inside). Hold in place with a couple of small stitches and, keeping the same needle and thread, start sewing the front and back together with an overhand stitch.

4 When you have sewn about three-quarters of the way, start filling your fish with the lavender. You can add a very small amount of toy stuffing in the pointed bits such as the tail and mouth if you want. Carry on stitching and add a bit more lavender or toy stuffing before closing completely.

Racoon & Fox

These hanging decorations are so much fun to make and will be sure to raise smiles of delight. They look a little mischievous so do make sure you keep an eye on them! They will look great hanging on a wall, a door handle or in the car. You could also fill them with lavender.

1 Cut out the templates and transfer to the felt. You will need for the fox: two bodies, one tummy and one tail piece. For the racoon: two bodies, one tummy, one mask, two eyes and three strips of 0.5 x 2cm (¼ x ¾in). Cut the felt. When embroidering these projects, split your thread and use only two or three strands (see page 10).

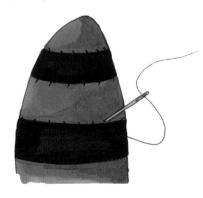

YOU WILL NEED

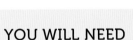

- Racoon & Fox body, tummy, mask, eyes and tail pieces (page 121)

MATERIALS (for both)

- Rusty brown and grey felt, at least 20 x 15cm (7¾ x 6in) each
- White felt, at least 10 x 15cm (4 x 6in)
- Black felt, at least 6 x 6cm (2¼ x 2¼in)
- Black and dark brown embroidery thread
- 40cm (16in) of thin ribbon or twine
- Toy stuffing, about 10g (⅓oz)

TOOLS

- Scissors (paper, fabric and embroidery)
- Pen or pencil
- Embroidery needle

2 Fox (dark brown thread)
Place the tummy piece on the front body and pin into place. Stitch the nose in a triangular shape with a few long stitches, catching the white felt of the tummy.

Make the whiskers with a few long stitches. Now you need to attach the rest of the tummy piece by stitching all the way round with small overhand stitches. Draw the eyes with a faint pencil line and use backstitch to work them.

Pin the tail end in place. This will be stitched when you sew the front and back together.

3 Racoon (black thread)
Place the tummy on the front body and pin into place. Stitch the nose in a triangular shape with a few long stitches and sew the mouth with backstitch (you can draw it first with a pencil line). Now you need to attach the rest of the tummy piece by stitching all the way round with small overhand stitches. Stitch the mask into place with a few small overhand stitches.

Place the eyes on top and attach with French knots to make the pupils. Make your racoon look forward or sideways for a more suspicious look! Attach the stripes on the tail with small overhand stitches. Trim off the ends to fit perfectly on the tail.

4 Fox and Racoon

Attach a 20cm (8in) length of ribbon made into a loop at the top of the back piece, between the ears (on the wrong side) with a couple of small stitches and place the front body on top. The ends of the ribbon will be sandwiched between front and back.

Attach the two parts of the body together with simple overhand or blanket stitch. Start filling the tail when you have sewn around it. Carry on stitching and fill the rest of the body before closing the gaps end your stitching with a knot.

Spring & Easter

These delightful projects are all about nature waking up at springtime. Use beautiful, soft and gentle pastel shades mixed together to give a fresh, clean and modern look to your home. Invite hens, chicks, bunnies, birds and butterflies into your home to celebrate the new season.

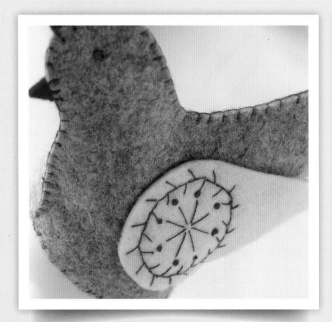

Hen Egg Cosies

Let these little hens keep your eggs warm for your Easter breakfast. They will look lovely displayed on your kitchen shelves the rest of the time and add a touch of Scandinavian style to your home. They are easy to make, and you could also fill them and close them at the bottom to make cute decorations instead.

YOU WILL NEED

- Hen, body, comb, beak and wing templates (page 117)

MATERIALS (per cosy)
- 1 piece of felt at least 21 x 19cm/8¼ x 7½in)
- 1 piece of felt for the wing at least 10 x 8cm (4 x 3¼in) – optional, if you want a contrasting wing
- Red felt at least 3 x 2cm (1¼ x ¾in)
- Red embroidery thread

TOOLS
- Scissors (paper, fabric and embroidery)
- Pen or pencil
- Embroidery needle
- Pins

1 Cut out the templates and transfer to the felt. You will need two bodies, two wings, one red comb and one red beak.

2 For best results, split your thread and use only one or two strands (see page 10). Pin the wing on the body. There is no need to sew it on as it will be held in place by the embroidered motif. I have used mock feather stitch for the outer shape but you could also use backstitch. You can make a circle and leave the point of the wing sticking out or you can follow the shape of the wing. Add a star stitch, some French knots or a lazy daisy stitch (see page 15–19). Do this on each side of the body.

3 Embroider the eyes with a simple French knot.

4 Pin both sides together and place the comb and the beak in the right place, sandwiched between the two layers. Start sewing together with blanket stitch, starting from the bottom and going all the way round to the other side. When you get to the beak and the comb, be sure to stitch through all three layers.

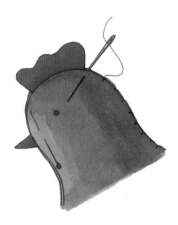

Do not close the bottom, but edge both sides with the same blanket stitch.

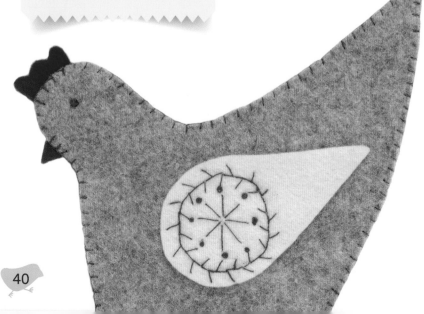

Bird Hanging

This was inspired by the beautiful traditional Indian bird hangings made using vibrant silks and embroidery. You could also make these birds as single hanging decorations or fill them with lavender.

1 Cut out the templates and transfer to the felt. You will need to cut in each colour two bodies and two wings so you will have ten in total. You can now decide how to mix them and which colour wing to give to each bird. Split your thread and use two strands (see page 10).

2 For each bird, sew the wing onto the body with running or backstitch about 3mm (⅛in) from the edge. Changing the colour of thread, embroider the wing shape, going smaller and smaller until you reach the middle where you can make a single daisy stitch. It is up to you how close together these embroidered shapes are: I found that four or five were enough. Do this for both sides of the birds.

4 To form a hanging loop for the top of the garland, fold 10cm (4in) of the ribbon length down and tie a knot. Position the spacing of your birds by placing one side of each bird (right side facing down) on your work surface in the order you want them. Make sure you space them out evenly (about 20cm/8in) apart). Position the ribbon through the middle (with the loop at the top) and place the matching sides of each bird on top of all backs, wrong sides together so the ribbon is sandwiched in between. Pin to hold in place, and sew each decoration with blanket stitch.

YOU WILL NEED

- Bird body and wing templates (page 122)

MATERIALS (for 5 birds)
- 5 pieces of felt, at least 15 x 15cm (6 x 6in) each in different shades
- Contrasting embroidery thread (3 colours minimum)
- 130cm (51½in) of ribbon
- Toy stuffing, 25g (1oz)
- Glass beads or sequins (optional)

TOOLS
- Scissors (paper, fabric and embroidery)
- Pen or pencil
- Pins
- Embroidery needle

3 Make a French knot for the eye and a little circle of backstitches around it. You could also use a bead or a sequin to add sparkle.

Add a little toy stuffing in each bird before closing completely and make sure you stitch through the ribbon each time.

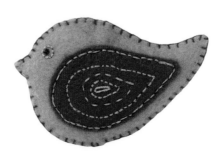

Easter Decorations

This mother hen looks really busy running after her chicks while keeping an eye on her eggs! Make as many as you want and hang them on a wreath or some twigs in a vase, or string them together as a garland. They make delightful little gifts you could give with chocolate eggs. They are simple and quick to make and are a perfect family craft project you can enjoy with children. Use fresh and soft pastel shades.

YOU WILL NEED

- Hen, chick, wings, comb, beak and egg templates (page 119)

MATERIALS (for 1 hen, 3 chicks and 3 eggs)

- 4 pieces of felt in pastel colours at least 10 x 15cm (4 x 6in) each
- Red felt, 3 x 3cm (1¼ x 1¼in)
- Red embroidery thread and any other colours you wish
- 70cm (27½in) of thin satin ribbon
- 40cm (15¾in) of colourful thin twisted cord, rope braid or twine
- Toy stuffing, about 10g (⅓oz)
- Cord for legs

TOOLS

- Scissors (paper, fabric and embroidery)
- Pen or pencil
- Embroidery needle

1 Cut out the templates and transfer to the felt. You will need two bodies, two wings and one red comb and one beak for the hen. For each chick you will need two bodies and two wings as well as a beak. For each egg you will need two pieces. Think carefully about your colours.

2 When embroidering this project, split your thread and use only two or three strands (see page 10).

Hen and Chicks

3 Place the wing on the body and attach with French knots or lines of stitches to decorate it. Do this for the front and back. The illustration shows the chick, but you can make the hen in the same way.

4 Make the eye with a French knot. If you want a speckled hen, add a lot of little dots all over the body with French knots. Again do this for the front and back.

5 Fold a 10cm (4in) length of ribbon in half to form a loop and place the ends in the curve of the back piece (on the wrong side). Secure with a few small stitches and place the front body on top. The ends of the ribbon will be sandwiched between front and back. Attach the two parts of the body together with simple overhand or blanket stitch.

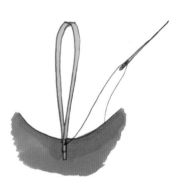

6 When you arrive at the top of the hen's head simply place the comb, sandwiched between the two body parts. Do the same for the beak for both hen and chicks, making sure you place enough of it in between the two body pieces so that it is held securely. You only need the little point showing as a beak.

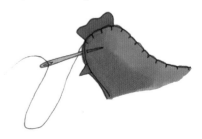

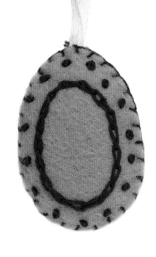

7 For the legs, cut a 10cm (4in) length of cord, make a knot at each end and fold in half. Insert the folded end between the front and back body pieces, catch with a few stitches and carry on sewing. Fill before closing completely.

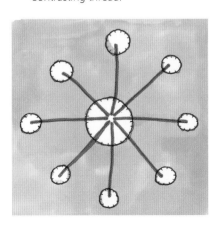

Eggs

8 Decorate both sides of the egg. You could make it stripy with lines of backstitches, or dotty with lots of French knots. You could also use a star or lazy-daisy stitch in the middle. The key is to use contrasting thread!

9 Attach the folded ribbon at the top sandwiched between the front and back (see step 5) and stitch all the way round. Blanket stitch looks great, but you could also use a simple overhand stitch.

Spring Hanging

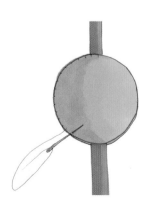

This hanging will bring spring freshness to your home with its soft pastel colours. It will look lovely hanging on a wall or a window. You could also make these circles as single decorations if you want to hang them on a few branches in a vase.

1 Cut out the templates and transfer to the felt. You will need to cut two large circles in each colour. Use the rest of the felt to cut one inner circle, one small and eight tiny ones, one flower and six leaves, one bird, one tree and one oval. Take five large circles (one of each colour) and decide which decoration you want to place on each one. Place the pieces of felt you will need on top of each one. Split your thread and use only one strand (see page 10).

YOU WILL NEED

- Circles, bird, flower, leaf, oval and tree foilage templates (page 122)

MATERIALS (for 5 birds)
- 5 pieces of felt at least 20 x 15cm (8 x 6in) each in different pastel shades
- Contrasting embroidery thread (3 colours minimum)
- 130cm (51¼in) of ribbon

TOOLS
- Scissors (paper, fabric and embroidery)
- Pen or pencil
- Pins
- Embroidery needle

2 The tree
Pin the tree piece on your circle and embroider a trunk and some branches with backstitch. Please note the trunk comes out onto the circle itself. Add a lot of little French knots to look like blossoms.

3 The bird
Stitch an inner circle onto the large one using French knots all the way round. Sew the bird in the middle with small stitches; add a French knot for his eye and long straight stitches for his legs and feet. Draw a wing with a soft pencil line, embroider it with backstitch and add lazy-daisy stitches inside the wing to resemble feathers.

4 The geometric flower shape
Pin the small circle in the middle and prepare the eight tiny circles to go around it. Make a very long star stitch going from the middle to the centre of a tiny circle placed about 1cm (½in) from the edge. Follow a + and then an X shape to space them out evenly. Add blanket stitch, in a matching thread, around the small circle and around each tiny circle to hold securely and to go over the thread of the long star stitch. Add French knots around each tiny circle.

5 The flower
Make a stem with two parallel lines of backstitches (about 2cm/¾in long). Add the leaves evenly on each side with a long straight stitch. Place the flower on top and sew with a few long stitches then add a few French knots at the top.

6 The blossom branch
Make two lines of backstitches going through the middle of the oval shape. Add a V at the top and a few lines of branches on each side with a V shape at the end. Place lots of French knots at the end of each branch in little clusters. Sew the oval shape onto the last circle with blanket stitch.

7 Fold 10cm (4in) of the ribbon and tie a knot to form a hanging loop. Place the five circles that have not been embroidered on your work surface in the order you want them. Add the ribbon through the middle with the loop at the top and place the embroidered circles on top, wrong sides together with the ribbon sandwiched in between.

Please note that it really adds to the design if you don't match the front and back circles but mix the colours.

Pin to hold in place, making sure you space them out evenly (about 20cm/8in apart) and sew each circle with blanket stitch. Make sure you stitch through the ribbon each time.

Butterfly & Flower Hanging

This hanging will bring a touch of summer into your home. Use some fresh pastel colours for a softer look or bright vibrant ones for a zestier one. It will look lovely hanging on a door or a wall in a bedroom or hallway. Feel free to add more embellishments with beads, sequins or buttons.

1 Cut out the templates and transfer to the felt. You will need two butterfly shapes, two wing pieces A and two of B and one body piece for each butterfly.

YOU WILL NEED

- Butterfly, body, wing pieces (A and B), large and small flower templates and flower centre (page 120)

MATERIALS
(2 butterflies and 3 flowers)

- 5 pieces of felt at least 20 x 15cm (8 x 6in) each, in different shades
- Contrasting embroidery thread (2 colours minimum)
- 150cm (59¼in) of ricrac ribbon or 3 pieces of 50cm (19¾in) in different colours
- Toy stuffing (optional)

TOOLS

- Scissors (paper, fabric and embroidery)
- Pen or pencil
- Pins
- Embroidery needle

For each flower, you will need two large flower shapes, one small flower and one flower centre. Think carefully about the colours you are mixing and layering together. When embroidering this project please split your thread and use only two or three strands (see page 10).

2 The butterfly
Place the decorative pieces A and B on the wings and hold in place with stitches such as French knots, running, backstitch or lazy daisy stitch.
Use contrasting colours of thread to make the embroidery part of the design. You could also add glass beads, sequins or small buttons. Place the body of the butterfly in the centre and hold with small overhand stitches or large straight stitches in the middle or even a line of French knots (you do not need to decorate the back piece).

3 The flower
Layer the circle and the smaller flower on top of the larger flower and use your preferred decorative stitches to hold in place. You could use French knots, lazy daisy, backstitch or long stitch. As for the butterfly, use a contrasting colour of thread and feel free to add beads, sequins or buttons. You do not need to decorate the back piece.

4 When you have decorated all the butterfly and flower front pieces, take the length of ribbon, leave about 30cm (12in) at the top, fold the end and tie a knot to form a loop. This will be the hanging loop at the top.

5 Place all the back pieces of the butterflies and flowers on your work surface in the order you want them, add the ribbon with the loop at the top and place the decorated front pieces on backs, wrong sides together with the ribbon sandwiched in between. If you decided to use three colours of ribbon, just place them one after the other as if they were one length.
   Pin in place and sew each decoration with blanket or overhand stitch. You can add a little toy stuffing if you wish but it is not necessary.

Decorative Rabbits

These little bunnies are adorable and will look great as a group. Place them on a shelf, the mantelpiece or your Easter table for a cute spring touch. I was inspired when at the local farm with my children and we saw a group of rabbits eating grass. They looked like they were having a little chat and a giggle!

YOU WILL NEED

- Rabbit body, rabbit tummy, ear pieces, top of the head and tail templates (page 117)

MATERIALS (per bunny)
- 1 piece of fur-coloured felt at least 20 x 15cm (8 x 6in) and 1 piece of white felt at least 10 x 15cm (4 x 6in)
- Dark brown embroidery thread
- 20cm (8in) of gingham or polka dot ribbon, 1cm (½in) wide
- Toy stuffing, 6g (¼oz)

TOOLS
- Scissors (paper, fabric and embroidery)
- Pen or pencil
- Embroidery needle

1 Cut out the templates and transfer to the felt. You will need two bodies, one head piece and two ears in the fur-coloured felt and one tummy, two inner ears and one tail in the white felt. Cut the felt.

For best results, I would advise splitting your thread and using only two or three strands as all the stitches will need to be small and delicate. See page 10 for advice.

2 Embroider the eyes and the whiskers on each side, using backstitch or simple long stitches.

3 Place the white inner ear on top of the coloured ear and stitch with small overhand stitches. Fold the base in half to give it a bit of depth and sew small overhand stitches along the base.

4 Place the top of the head piece onto one side of the body and start sewing with an overhand stitch from the nose point D, going up towards the top of the head.

When you reach the place for the ears, simply insert them with the white facing forward and carry on stitching through the side layer, the ear and the top of the head. Sew all the way to point C.

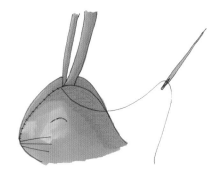

5 Position the other side of the body, matching points C and D and stitch from C to D. Do not forget to insert the other ear!

Sew the two body sides together at the chin from D to B.

6 Place a few straight stitches close together on the point of the nose. This will keep the end tidy and make a cute nose.

7 Add the tummy piece, matching the front and back legs to the body pieces. Stitch from point B and sew all the way to A on one side and then back to B on the other side.

   Fill your bunny with the toy stuffing, making sure it goes into the nose and legs to give them a nice shape. Close the body completely by sewing from A to C and adding a bit more toy stuffing if necessary.

8 To make the tail, close to the edge of the circle with a loose running stitch and don't cut the thread. Pull gently on the thread to gather the felt and form a ball shape. Place a small amount of toy stuffing inside and knot the ends of the thread. Attach the tail to the bunny's behind with small stitches all the way round. Finally, tie the ribbon around the bunny's neck and finish with a bow.

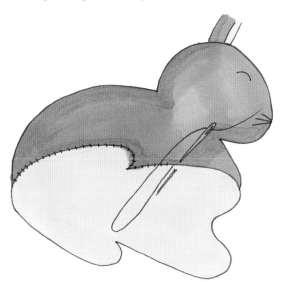

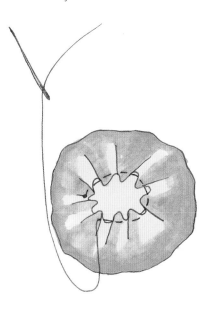

Autumn & Winter

These projects are perfect to decorate your home for the colder days. Think rich deep muted colours for an autumnal feel and of course red, light blue and white for a Scandinavian Christmas look.

Curl up near the fire with a warm beverage (don't forget to use your mug cosy) and your felt and threads to make all your favourite decorations for yourself or as special presents. What better way to spend a few hours as the nights are drawing in?

Christmas Lavender Bag

This hanging bag will look lovely on a door handle or on the wall. I filled mine with lavender but you could use cinnamon or cloves for a more festive feel. Try using the little bags sold to make mulled wine. They are filled with spices and safely packaged. This hanging bag can also be personalised with a name or message embroidered with backstitch.

1   Cut out the templates and transfer to the felt. You will need to cut two rectangles of 9 x 12cm (3½ x 4¾in) for the bag itself and one gingerbread man, two hearts and two stars.

YOU WILL NEED

- Gingerbread man, heart and star templates (page 116)

MATERIALS

- 20cm (7¾in) of ribbon
- Felt for the bag at least 18 x 12cm (7 x 4¾in)
- Felt for the gingerbread man at least 8 x 6cm (3¼ x 2¼in)
- White and red felt for the hearts and stars, 3 x 3cm (1¼ x 1¼in)
- Dark brown embroidery thread
- 5g (¼oz) of toy stuffing
- Dried lavender flowers, 15g (½oz)
- Small buttons or beads (optional)

TOOLS

- Scissors (paper, fabric and embroidery)
- Pen or pencil
- Embroidery needle

2   For best results, split your thread and use only one or two strands (see page 10). Place your gingerbread man on one of the rectangles of felt and sew with blanket stitch. Make little curves for his eyes and mouth with backstitch. Add three cross stitches or French knots down his front or alternatively use real buttons.

3   Draw a curve above his head, going from one hand to the other, with a faint pencil line and embroider with thick backstitch (use three strands for this).

4   Add the stars and hearts and hold in place with a few stitches. You could use running or backstitch for this. Alternatively you could use buttons or beads in the shape of stars and hearts.
   If you wish to add a name, date or message, do so now either on the front or the back piece. Backstitch is ideal for this.

5   Once you are happy with the front, fold the ribbon in half to form a loop and place the ends on the wrong side of the back piece at the top. Stitch in place. Do not cut your thread – simply position the front piece on top of the back piece with the ribbon ends sandwiched in between. Stitch round with blanket stitch, leaving a small gap to fill.

6   Add a bit of toy stuffing at the bottom and then some lavender. You can add another small layer of toy stuffing at the top to seal everything in. Carry on stitching until you get back to where you started. Make a secure knot and cut your thread.

Woodland Mobile

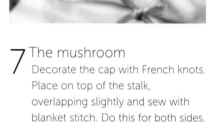

Bring the woods into your home with all their poetry and magic! This mobile will look great on twigs in a vase or on a branch hanging on the wall. You could also use a willow circle (like a wreath) to hang the decorations from and make a mobile to hang from the ceiling.

1 Cut out the templates and transfer to the felt. You will need to cut two of each template. Cut more if you are making an item more than once.

YOU WILL NEED

- All woodland templates: tree, leaf, acorn nut and cup, mushroom cap and stalk, flower top and leaves, bird and wing, squirrel, owl body and wing and hedgehog body and face (page 125)

MATERIALS

- A minimum of 10 pieces of felt in woodland colours, 10 x 15cm (4 x 6in) each. Include browns, greens, oranges but also red and white. Use small scraps you might have too.

- 4 or more shades of embroidery thread (red, brown, white, blue)

- 20cm (8in) of thin ribbon for each decoration

- 40cm (16in) of colourful thin twisted cord, rope braid or twine

- Toy stuffing, about 10g (⅓oz)

TOOLS

- Scissors (paper, fabric and embroidery)

- Pen or pencil

- Embroidery needle

2 Split your thread and use only one strand (see page 10). Please note: for all decorations, apart from the owl, follow the instructions below for both sides.

3 The tree
Add a few straight stitches to look like branches and some French knots.

4 The leaf
Make a few lines of backstitches to look like the veins of a leaf.

5 The flower
Decorate the flower top with long straight stitches and French knots. Place on top of the stem, overlapping slightly and attach with blanket stitch. Do this for both sides.

6 The acorn
Place the cup on top of the nut (lower part), overlapping slightly and sew together with blanket stitch. Add French knots on the cup to give texture.

7 The mushroom
Decorate the cap with French knots. Place on top of the stalk, overlapping slightly and sew with blanket stitch. Do this for both sides.

8 The owl
Add the wings on the side and fill with lines of running stitches. Cut two small circles for the eyes and attach to the body with a star stitch (leaving a gap in the middle). Add a French knot as the pupil. Embroider a beak with a few long stitches close together. Only the front part of the body is to be decorated.

9 The bird

Place the wing on the body and sew with running stitch round the edge. Make a few more lines of running and backstitches, following the same shape and going smaller. Add a small circle of felt or two on top of each other and sew with a star stitch for the eye.

10 The hedgehog

Place the face on the body and add a French knot for the eye. Add lines of running stitches to look like spines. When you have joined the front and back together as explained in step 12, make a few stitches close together on the end of the nose.

11 The squirrel

Fill the tail with a few lines of running stitches. Add a French knot for the eye. When you have joined the front and back as explained in step 12, add a few stitches at the end of the nose.

12

Stitch the end of a 20cm (8in) length of ribbon at the top of one side of each decoration, add the other side on top (so that the ribbon is sandwiched between the two pieces of felt) and sew together with blanket stitch.

13

Now tie the ribbon on each decoration to your chosen item (branch, twigs or a circular base). It adds to the project if you hang the decorations at different heights.

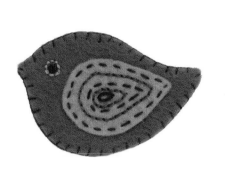

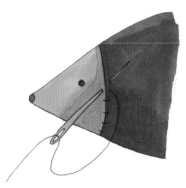

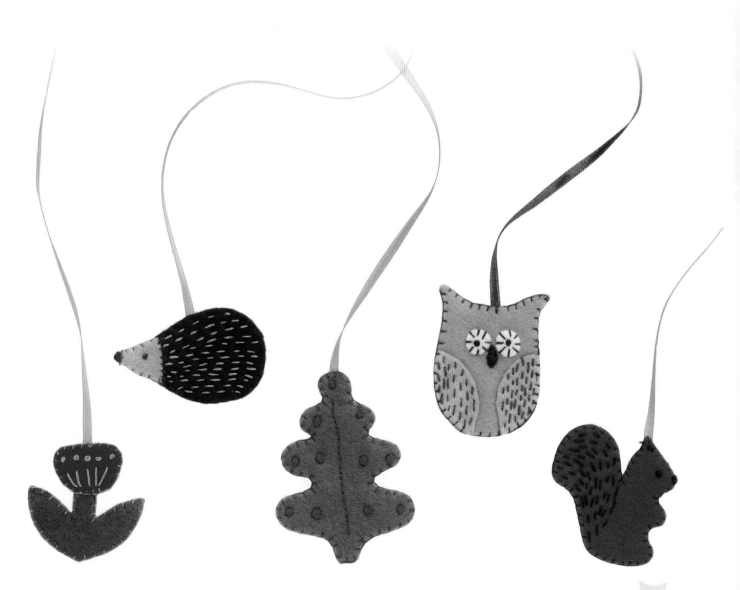

Halloween Decorations

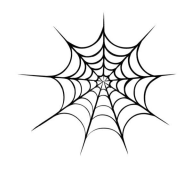

The local witch is getting ready for Halloween and has done her washing to look her best! She is probably in the bath while it is all drying! This project will look like bunting once you peg all the items on the twine. Hang it in your window to make trick-or-treaters smile. Add a few plastic spiders and fake cobwebs to create the right atmosphere.

YOU WILL NEED

- All Halloween templates: dress, hat, bloomers, cat, cat's face, shoe and stocking (page 126)

MATERIALS
- Black felt, at least 25 x 20cm (10 x 8in)
- Orange and white felt, at least 10 x 5cm (4 x 2in)
- Black, orange and white embroidery thread
- 10cm (4in) of thin orange satin ribbon for the hat
- 50cm (20in) of twine and 8 mini wooden pegs

TOOLS
- Scissors (paper, fabric and embroidery)
- Pen or pencil
- Embroidery needle

1 Cut out the templates and transfer to the felt. You will need to cut two of each item but only one cat face plus four stockings and four shoes. Make sure you only cut the curve in the neckline of the dress for the front.

2 Split your thread and use only one strand (see page 10). Work as follows:

The dress
Place the front onto the back and sew the side seams and sleeves with blanket stitch in orange. Blanket stitch the neckline too.

The bloomers
Add orange French knots all over. Sew the front and back together with blanket stitch, leaving the waist and bottom of the legs open. Use three strands of thread to tie around the knees with a bow. Trim off the ends.

The shoes
Sew front and back together and add a bow for the laces with two or three strands of thread.

The hat
Sew the front and back together with blanket stitch. Place the ribbon around the base, cross the ends over and stitch in place. Trim the ends with a V shape as shown.

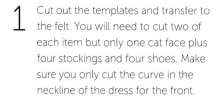

The cat

Place the face on top of the front body. Attach with white blanket stitch. Add French knots for the eyes and nose and a few small stitches for the mouth. Sew the front and back together with blanket stitch.

The stockings

Stitch the front and back together with blanket stitch. With a length of full-thickness thread, sew through the two layers (front and back) to create the stripes, a little bit like long straight stitches parallel to each other. Leave the heel plain and hide the ends inside.

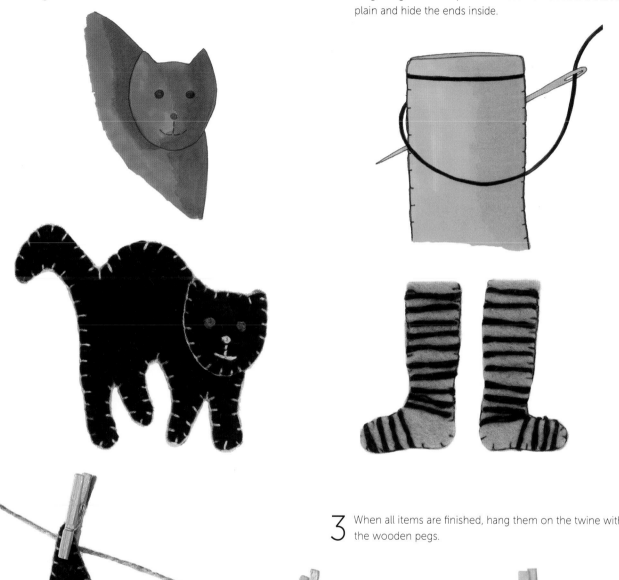

3 When all items are finished, hang them on the twine with the wooden pegs.

Christmas Pixie

Make your very own little pixie to help you get ready for the festive season but remember that pixies do not like to be alone so be sure to make him a few friends too. Place them on you mantelpiece, under the tree, on your windowsill or the Christmas table. They will certainly delight children and grown-ups alike and make a lovely gift too.

1 Cut out the templates and transfer to the felt. You will need two bodies, one base and four arms in blue, one hat and four hands in red. Cut a rectangle of felt of 5 x 12cm (2 x 4¾in) for the face.

YOU WILL NEED

- Pixie body, base, hat, arm and hand templates (page 124)

MATERIALS

- Light blue or turquoise felt, at least 20 x 15cm (7¾ x 6in)
- Red felt, 15 x 15cm (6 x 6in)
- Beige felt, 12 x 5cm (4¾ x 2in)
- Dark brown, white, red and blue embroidery thread
- Toy stuffing, about 20g (1 oz)
- Dried lentils or uncooked rice (a handful)

TOOLS

- Scissors (paper, fabric and embroidery)
- Pen or pencil
- Embroidery needle
- Fabric glue (optional)

2 Split your thread to use only one strand (see page 10).

Start with a straight line of running stitches through the middle of one body piece. This will be the front. Sew front and back together with small overhand stitches along the sides. Place the base at the bottom (largest side) and attach with blanket stitch.

3 Sew each hand to an arm piece with blanket stitch. Take two arm/hand pieces and sew together with blanket stitch, adding some toy stuffing before closing completely.

Sew the top of the arms to the sides of the body. Don't worry too much about the neatness as this will be hidden by the hat.

4 Take the rectangle of beige felt. Find the middle – this will be the face. Use the hat template as a guide to see how big the face needs to be. It needs to fill the hat opening in the base. Draw curves for eyes and mouth onto the beige felt and embroider with a backstitch.

Close the rectangle on the shorter edges (to form a cylinder) with small stitches. Place this cylinder at the top of the body, with the blue felt overlapping the beige, making sure the features are at the front; and attach with running or blanket stitch all the way round. Fill the body with the lentils or rice to give it weight and then with toy stuffing. Tie a piece of thread at the top to close it, a little bit like a sack.

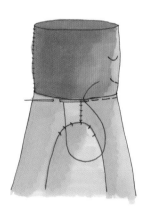

5 Embroider the bottom edge of the hat with mock feather stitch and close the back (to form a cone) with a small overhand stitch. Add a little toy stuffing in the pointed end to keep the shape and place the hat on top of the head, making sure the face shows through the opening. You can now glue the hat on with a small amount of fabric glue or stitch it on with small red stitches going through the head (it will not hurt your pixie!).

Scandi Houses

These Scandinavian-style houses look great in neutral, natural colours but they could also be made with brighter colours for a completely different look. Filled with lavender they are both beautiful and practical and will make delightful gifts.

1 Cut out the templates and transfer to the felt. You will need two walls, two roofs and one door.

YOU WILL NEED

- Wall, roof and door templates (page 122)

MATERIALS (for 1 house)
- 20cm (8in) of ribbon
- Felt for the walls (approximately 15 x 10cm/ 6 x 4in)
- Felt for the roof and door, 15 x 8cm (6 x 3¼in)
- White felt for the windows, 3 x 3cm (1¼ x 1¼in) optional
- Contrasting embroidery thread
- 5g (¼oz) of toy stuffing
- Dried lavender flowers, 15g (½oz)

TOOLS
- Scissors (paper, fabric and embroidery)
- Pen or pencil
- Embroidery needle

2 I would advise splitting your thread and using only one strand as all the stitches will need to be small and delicate (see page 10)

Sew the door on the front wall with backstitch about 3mm (⅛in) from the edge. You could add a French knot for the door knob, if you wish.

3 For the windows you can draw four 1.5cm (⅝in) squares with a very faint pencil line. A good way to make sure they are lined up is to fold the wall piece along the middle (vertically) and to measure 0.5cm (¼in) from the line for each window. Embroider the windows with backstitch. Add a cross in the middle with backstitch or long straight stitches. Alternatively, you can cut four 1.5cm (⅝in) felt squares and place them on the wall. Attach them with long straight stitches close to the edges and a cross in the middle.

4 Place the roof piece on top of the wall, overlapping slightly and sew with blanket or backstitch along the lower edge. Do this for the front and back.

5 Take the ribbon and fold into a loop. Attach the ends inside the pointed bit of the roof of the back piece with a couple of small stitches.

6 Place the front and back together (right side out) and start stitching from the top all the way round with blanket or backstitch. Leave a gap large enough for you to fill the house with ¼ toy stuffing at the bottom, lavender flowers in the middle and ¼ toy stuffing again at the top of the roof. Carry on stitching to close the gap.

Mug Cosy

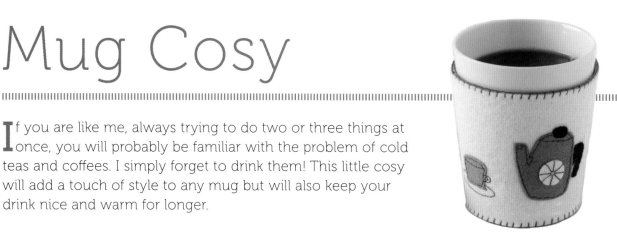

If you are like me, always trying to do two or three things at once, you will probably be familiar with the problem of cold teas and coffees. I simply forget to drink them! This little cosy will add a touch of style to any mug but will also keep your drink nice and warm for longer.

YOU WILL NEED

- Cosy, coffee pot, handle, lid knob and cup templates (page 125)

MATERIALS (per cosy)
- White and golden orange felt, at least 30 x 15cm (12 x 6in)
- Moss and black felt, at least 5 x 5cm (2 x 2in)
- Brown embroidery thread
- 15cm (6in) of thin colourful elastic cord
- 2 buttons

TOOLS
- Scissors (paper, fabric and embroidery)
- Pen or pencil
- Pins
- Embroidery needle

1 Cut out the templates and transfer to the felt, remembering to use the fold line. You will need two cosy shapes (one white, one orange), one coffee pot in moss, one handle and lid knob in black and a cup in orange. Please note that you can adjust the size of the cosy if it doesn't fit your mug. Do it on the template before cutting the felt!

2 Split your thread and use only one strand (see page 10).

Place the coffee pot on the white felt and stitch all the way round with a backstitch. Add a curved line to look like a lid and fix the knob on top with a few small stitches. Add the handle on the side in the same manner. Cut a small white circle of felt (about 1.5cm/⁵⁄₈ in) and sew onto the coffee pot with a star stitch.

Sew the cup on the white felt, next to the coffee pot, with a backstitch going round the edges. Add a curve to show the opening of the cup and a handle going out onto the white felt. Stitch an oval shape at the bottom of the cup to look like a saucer in the same manner. You can draw it first with a faint pencil line.

3 Cut the elastic cord in half and tie knots to form two loops. Pin them on the edge of the orange felt as shown below, about 1.5cm (⁵⁄₈ in) from the top and bottom.

Place the white felt on top so that the knots of the elastic cord loops are sandwiched between the two pieces of felt. Sew all the way round with blanket stitch, making sure you catch the elastic loops a few times to secure them.

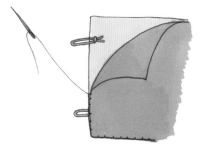

4 Place the cosy around your mug and see where the buttons need to be to fit in the elastic loops without pulling too much. Stitch in place and make yourself a nice cup of coffee!

Heart Hanging

This felt embroidered heart is great for practising your embroidery stitches. It can be filled with lavender or toy stuffing and will look good just about anywhere in the house. It can make a lovely gift for your Valentine. You could add a message, name or date on the back with simple backstitch. It would also make a wedding present with a personalised message to the bride and groom.

1 Cut out the template and transfer to the felt. You will need to cut two heart shapes.

For all your embroidery I would advise splitting the thread and using only two strands.

YOU WILL NEED

- Heart template (page 116)

MATERIALS
- 1 piece of white felt, (20 x 32cm/ 8 x 12½in)
- Red embroidery thread
- 40cm (16in) of thin red satin ribbon
- Toy stuffing (20g/1oz) or loose dried lavender flowers (about 30g/1oz)
- Glass beads

TOOLS
- Scissors (paper, fabric and embroidery)
- Pen or pencil
- Embroidery needle

2 You use the design here, create your own or follow the example on the template provided on page 116. Use the technique shown on page 11 to transfer the embroidery pattern to the felt. You can do this even if you are using your own design; simply draw on the tissue paper.

3 Embroider through the tissue paper and the felt at the same time. When you have finished, tear off the tissue, making sure you remove all small pieces very gently so you do not disturb the stitches.

4 You can leave the back piece blank or add a message, a date or a name in backstitch.

5 Fold 10cm (4in) of the ribbon to form a loop and place the end at the top of the back piece (on the wrong side) with the other end of the ribbon hanging down at the bottom. Make a couple of straight stitches to hold in place at the top. Do not cut the thread.

6 Place the front onto the back and stitch all the way round with blanket stitch. Make sure you leave the ribbon hanging at the bottom.

When you are about three-quarters of the way round, fill the heart with toy stuffing or alternatively place a little bit of toy stuffing in the point at the bottom and fill the rest with lavender.

Carry on stitching until you reach the top again. Secure with a knot.

7 Add the beads onto the ribbon at the bottom and knot the end to hold securely in place. You can also slip a bead onto the ribbon above the heart as a finishing touch.

Christmas Clog & Mitten

These two decorations will really bring a Scandinavian touch to your home. They are relatively simple to make and only require a small amount of felt, so you could make quite a few and hang them on your tree or string them together as bunting. As they are open at the top, you can hide little surprises inside. They would be ideal for an advent calendar.

1 Cut out the templates and transfer to the felt. You will need to cut two red clog shapes, two red mittens and two white cuffs. For all the embroidery use only one strand (see page 10).

YOU WILL NEED

- Clog, mitten and cuff templates (page 117)

MATERIALS (for 1 clog and 1 mitten)

- 1 piece of red felt, at least 15 x 20cm (6 x 7¾in)

- 1 piece of white felt, 6 x 5cm (2¼ x 2in)

- White embroidery thread

- 30cm (12in) of thin white ricrac ribbon

TOOLS

- Scissors (paper, fabric and embroidery)

- Pen or pencil

- Embroidery needle

2 Use mock feather stitch and some French knots to decorate the mitten on the front only and the clog on both sides. Follow the design shown in the photograph or create your own. You can draw with a pen on the felt to trace your design first if you want. For the clog, make sure your design matches from one side to the other. If you are making the circle as shown on the photograph for example, it needs to be symmetrical to create a prefect circle on what will be the front of the clog.

3 Attach the white cuff at the top of the mitten with a line of backstitches.

4 Cut 15cm (6in) of ribbon and fold in half to form a loop. Place the ends on the inside of the back piece as shown below (on the side of the cuff for the mitten and on the back of the ankle for the clog). Hold with a few small stitches. Do not cut the thread.

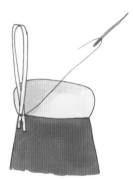

5 Place the front onto the back and stitch all the way round with blanket stitch. Do this for both decorations. For the mitten, start stitching on the side of the white cuff all the way down and to the other side. Leave the top open, as for a real mitten.

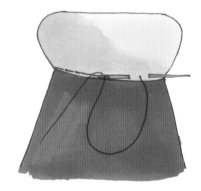

For the clog, start stitching at the back of the ankle, down to the heel and back up to the pointed end. Carry on to the front of the ankle and leave open at the top, as for a real shoe. You can finish the open edges with blanket stitch.

6 If you do not want to hide surprises in your decorations, you can add a very small amount of toy stuffing at the bottom to give them a fuller shape.

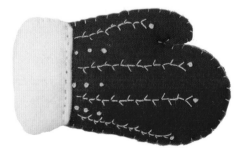

Scandi Horse

I have always been fascinated by traditional folk craft, especially from Scandinavia. I love the quality of craftsmanship and timeless properties of it. The Dala horse is a traditional carved painted wooden figure from Sweden and I thoroughly enjoyed making it in felt, keeping the 3D standing properties. This little horse will look fabulous on your windowsill, mantelpiece or Christmas table. It will be a hit with both children and grownups but do be careful not to let young children play with it because of the small decorative pieces.

YOU WILL NEED

- Horse body, underside, circle and petal-shaped templates (page 119)

MATERIALS
- 1 piece of dark red felt, at least 22 x 30cm (8¾ x 12in)
- White felt, 10 x 10cm (4 x 4in)
- Red, blue and yellow embroidery thread and any other colours you wish
- Toy stuffing, about 30g (1oz)

TOOLS
- Scissors (paper, fabric and embroidery)
- Pen or pencil
- Pins
- Embroidery needle

1 Cut out the templates and transfer to the felt. You will need two bodies and one underside in the red felt and six circles and eight petal shapes in the white. Cut the felt.

2 Split your embroidery thread following the technique on page 10 and use only one or two strands. Position your cut-out shapes on the body following the picture and sew into place with running stitch in the middle of the petal shapes and with a large star stitch or simple straight stitches for the circles.

3 Make the eyes with long stitches close together and decorate the rest of the body with lazy daisy stitches and French knots. You can also make the tail with lines of running stitch or backstitches.
Make sure you decorate both body pieces in the same way.

4 Once you are happy with the body of your horse, you can sew the pieces together. Start by folding the underside in half, lengthways, and place it between the two sides of the horse, matching the legs with the corners of the underside template. Pin in place.

5 Use a simple overhand or blanket stitch to attach the underside to the body. Your horse should have four legs you can fill to make him stand up.

6 Carry on sewing up to the neck, round the head to the withers. Fill the head and neck and finish sewing the back, filling your horse before closing completely.

Home & lifestyle

Invite special friends from the woodland into your home and they will be sure to make you smile every day! These pieces make ideal presents for adults, children and new parents but you might want to keep them for yourself and make them part of your family. Use wool felt in a mix of natural warm colours for a soft, snuggly look.

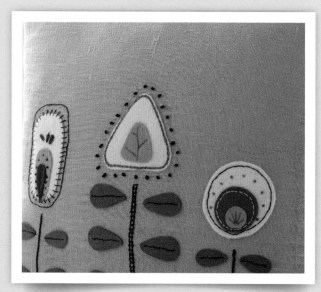

Bag Charm

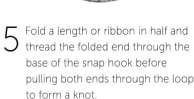

These bag charms are simple yet eye-catching – the secret is in using beautiful shades of felt and ribbons. But don't stop there, use them for key rings and hanging decorations, enlarge them to make coasters or string them together to make a garland.

1 Cut out the templates and transfer to the felt. You will need two red circles, one soft green and one turquoise, one white mushroom stalk and wall, one red roof and mushroom cap and one dark green tree piece. Cut a small rectangle of 1 x 0.8cm (½ x ³/₈in) in the red felt for the door.

2 Split your embroidery thread (see page 10) and use only one strand. Sew the mushroom stalk on the green circle with small white stitches. Add the mushroom cap (overlapping slightly at the top of the stalk) and make a lot of white French knots.

5 Fold a length or ribbon in half and thread the folded end through the base of the snap hook before pulling both ends through the loop to form a knot.

YOU WILL NEED

- Circle, mushroom cap and stalk, house (roof and wall) and tree templates (page 124)

MATERIALS
(for two bag charms)
- Soft green, turquoise and white felt at least 7 x 7cm (2¾ x 2¾in)
- Red felt, 10 x 15cm (4 x 6in)
- Dark green felt, 2.5 x 2cm (1 x ¾in)
- 2 lengths of ribbon of 30cm (12in)
- 2 snap hooks, about 4cm/1½in high, or to fit your bag; I used antique bronze hooks
- Red, white and brown embroidery thread and any other colours you wish to include

TOOLS
- Scissors (paper, fabric and embroidery)
- Pen or pencil
- Embroidery needle

3 Sew the white wall on the blue circle; add the red roof and the door with matching small stitches. Use long straight stitches to make the squares for the windows

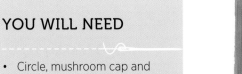

4 Embroider a line of about 1cm (½in) with backstitch in brown to make the tree trunk, add the green tree piece and sew straight stitches through it to resemble branches.

6 Sew the ends of the ribbon to the red circle of felt with a few small stitches. Place one of the decorated circles on top (ribbon ends sandwiched between the two pieces) and sew together all the way round with blanket stitch. Repeat for the other bag charm.

Russian Doll

I love Russian dolls and my favourite thing about them is the way you open them until you find the very last one who is so small and adorable and a perfect replica of the larger ones. My felt doll was inspired by this so there is a little doll that looks just like the big one. It is also the perfect image of a mother and her baby and it will make a delightful gift for someone who is expecting or has just had a baby. You can personalise your doll and embroider a name, a date or a wish for the new arrival. You can put the baby in the mother's pocket or hide a little surprise, a token or a message there.

YOU WILL NEED

- Large doll's body and base templates and small doll's body template (page 118)

MATERIALS
- Felt for the large doll's body, at least 40 x 32cm (16 x 12½in)
- Felt for the pocket and flower, 20 x 15cm (8 x 6in)
- Felt for the baby, 20 x 15cm (8 x 6in)
- Beige felt, 10 x 15cm (4 x 6in)
- Dark brown, pink or red and white embroidery thread
- Toy stuffing, about 80g (3oz)
- Ribbon, beads, buttons (optional)

TOOLS
- Scissors (paper, fabric and embroidery)
- Pen or pencil
- Pins
- Embroidery needle

1 Cut out the templates and transfer to the felt. You will need two large bodies, one base and two small bodies. You also need to cut the pocket for the large doll as a rectangle of 10 x 19cm (4 x 7½in) and two squares for the faces (10 x 10cm/4 x 4in for the large doll and 5 x 5cm/2 x 2in for the small one). Please note that when you are cutting the body pieces you should only cut out the circle for the face on one side, which will be the front!

2 Split your thread to use only two strands (see page 10). Starting with the large doll, place the square of beige felt under the circular hole you have cut into the front body piece and pin in place. Sew all the way round the face to attach together with backstitch or blanket stitch. Once securely stitched in place you can trim the beige felt at the back to fit within the shape of the doll.

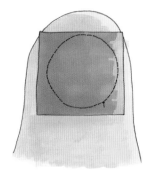

3 Embroider the features of the face. Draw them first with a pencil. You can use backstitch for the eyes and the mouth and long straight stitches close together for the pupils. Think of the expression you want your doll to have. You can also add hair or freckles with French knots.

4 Decorate the pocket with embroidery (you could add stars, flowers, dots) or attach ribbon, beads or buttons. You can also decorate the dress if you wish. If you want to personalise your doll with a name or a message, you can embroider it on the pocket with backstitch. I would suggest tracing it lightly with a pencil first.

5 Place the front body onto the back and the pocket on top. Pin together and, starting from the bottom, stitch all the way round with blanket stitch until you reach the other side.

Fill your doll and sew on the base to close it completely.

6 Make the small doll in the same manner except that there is no pocket and no oval base to sew on.

7 Add a flower or a ribbon tied into a bow to your dolls if you wish. To make the flower as shown in the photo, simply cut a strip of felt of about 20 x 4cm (8 x 1½in). Snip the felt as shown in the drawing, at regular intervals of about 1cm (½in) and 3cm (1¼in) deep.

The uncut edge becomes the base; simply roll it as tightly as possible and glue or stitch securely. Sew or glue the base of the flower in your doll's hair and open out the cut strips to look more like a flower.

8 When you have finished, your small doll will live happily in the big doll's pocket!

Sleepy Fox Brooch

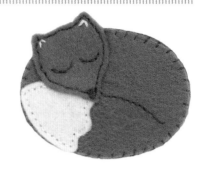

I love brooches so much. They will add a touch of colour or fun to any outfit. You can wear them on coats, cardigans, hats, scarves, shawls...just about anything! This sleepy fox is a miniature version of the fox pillow on page 98 and you can take him with you wherever you go. It will also make an adorable present and it is very quick to make.

1 Cut out the templates and transfer to the felt. You should have two body pieces, one head and one tail.

YOU WILL NEED

- Fox body, head and tail templates (page 116)

MATERIALS
- Rust brown felt at least 15 x 10cm (6 x 4in)
- White felt, 5 x 5cm (2 x 2in)
- Dark brown and white embroidery thread
- Brooch pin

TOOLS
- Scissors (paper, fabric and embroidery)
- Pen or pencil
- Embroidery needle
- Fabric glue (optional)

2 Split your thread to use only one strand (see page 10). Place the tail on one of the body pieces and stitch in place with backstitch. Following the top line of the tail, draw a continuation onto the rust brown felt as a curved line. Embroider with backstitch in brown.

3 Add the head at a slight angle with the top sticking out a little. Sew in place with backstitch all the way round. Make the eyes as little curves to look sleepy with backstitch again and add a few straight stitches close together on the nose. You can work an upside down V-shape in white on the ears if you want.

4 Take the back body piece and sew the brooch pin on the back with a few stitches going through the holes of the pin. Alternatively, you might prefer to glue it on.

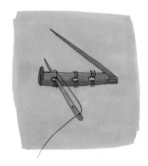

5 Place the front body onto the back and sew round with blanket stitch.

Scandi-Style Pillow

The perfect project to learn some simple, yet effective, appliqué techniques. The fun is in choosing your colours and mixing them. Keep the shapes simple and geometric and stick to three or four colours for a fresh, modern Scandinavian look. This project would work really well on a plain cotton tote bag too.

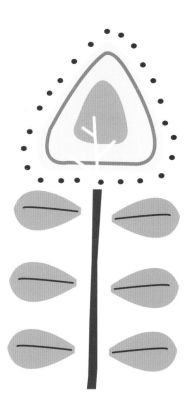

YOU WILL NEED

- Oblongs, rounded triangles, teardrop, circles and leaf templates (page 127)

MATERIALS

- 1 plain linen or cotton pillow cover + 1 inner pad
- Pieces of felt in 3 or 4 colours (approximately 20 x 15cm/ 8 x 6in each)
- 2 or 3 colours of embroidery thread thread

TOOLS

- Scissors (paper, fabric and embroidery)
- Pen or pencil
- Pins
- Embroidery needle
- Paper

1 Think carefully about the design you want to create and draw a sketch of it on a piece of paper. If you are using a rectangular cushion cover you could perhaps have five flowers next to each other or three in the middle. Cut out the templates and transfer to the felt. You can keep the templates as they are or enlarge and reduce them to create new layers of shapes. For the flower made with circles, for example, I used three different sizes of circle and layered them. Cut six to ten leaves per flower depending on the length of the stem.

2 Split your thread to use three or four strands (see page 10). Start by placing the base of each flower on the pillow cover and pin in place. By the base I mean the largest shape (white felt on my cushion). Be sure to open the cover and to pin and stitch only through the top layer! Sew the base pieces onto the cover using blanket, running or backstitch. You could also use long straight stitches. The stitching is a big part of the design in this project so it needs to be bold enough to stand out.

3 Now embroider the stems as long straight lines. Leave a gap between the flower and the stem. You can use backstitch or two parallel lines of backstitches with straight stitches between them, as in my middle flower.

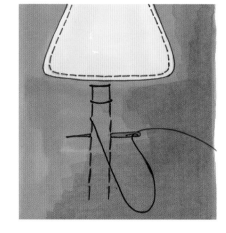

4 Pin the leaves in place at regular intervals on each side of the stems and sew with backstitch going through the middle of each leaf.

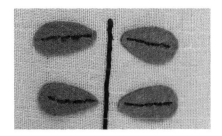

5 Now you can add layers to your flower bases. It works really well to use the same shape but smaller, for example a smaller triangle on top of a larger one. Attach each new shape with the stitches of your choice: blanket, back, running or long stitches. Add a few more details on each shape or around the base (directly onto the cushion cover) using the same stitches and also a few French knots. Be sure to end all your embroidery with secure knots inside the cover. When you have finished, place the pad inside the cover and close.

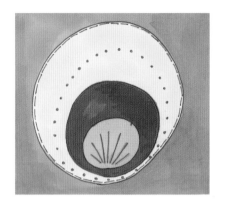

Owl Pillow

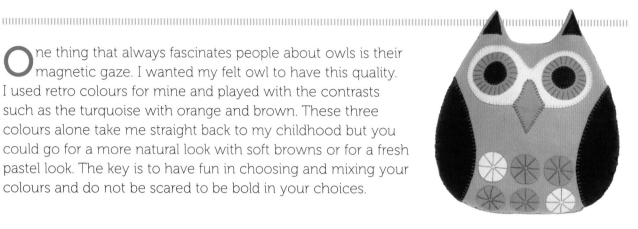

One thing that always fascinates people about owls is their magnetic gaze. I wanted my felt owl to have this quality. I used retro colours for mine and played with the contrasts such as the turquoise with orange and brown. These three colours alone take me straight back to my childhood but you could go for a more natural look with soft browns or for a fresh pastel look. The key is to have fun in choosing and mixing your colours and do not be scared to be bold in your choices.

YOU WILL NEED

MATERIALS
- Owl body, eye piece, eye, pupil, beak, ear and wing templates (page 120)

MATERIALS
- Turquoise felt, at least 70 x 35cm (27½ x 13¾in)
- White felt, 30 x 15cm (12 x 6in)
- Orange felt, 10 x 15cm (4 x 6in)
- Golden yellow felt, 16 x 15cm (6¼ x 6in)
- Brown felt, 30 x 20cm (12 x 8in)
- Dark turquoise and yellow embroidery thread
- Toy stuffing, about 100g (3½oz)

TOOLS
- Scissors (paper, fabric and embroidery)
- Pen or pencil
- Pins
- Embroidery needle

1 Cut out the templates and transfer to the felt. You will need two bodies in the turquoise, two wings, two ears and two pupils in brown, one eye piece in white, two yellow eyes, one orange beak and two pupil circles each in white, orange and yellow.

2 Split your thread to use only two or three strands (see page 10). Start by placing the large white eye piece onto the front body and secure with regular straight stitches or blanket stitch. Please note that in this project the stitches need to be quite big and bold as they become part of the design.

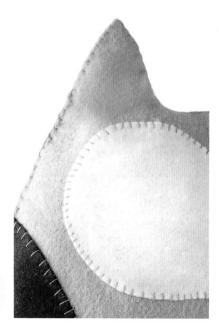

3 Now place the yellow eyes on top and centre them. Hold in place with very large straight stitches (about 1.5cm/ ⅝in). Place the brown pupils on top, centre them and hold with overhand or blanket stitch.

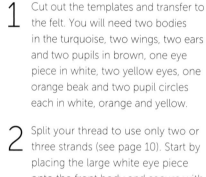

4 Place the beak between the eyes and sew with overhand stitches or blanket stitch. Do the same thing with the ears.

5 Pin the wings on the sides and sew only along the inner edge with overhand stitches, leaving the outer edge unstitched. Place your six circles in two rows of three at the bottom and pin. Use a large star stitch to keep in place.

6 You can now place the front onto the back and sew together with blanket stitch. When you get to the wings, make sure you are sewing though all three layers. Fill the owl before closing completely.

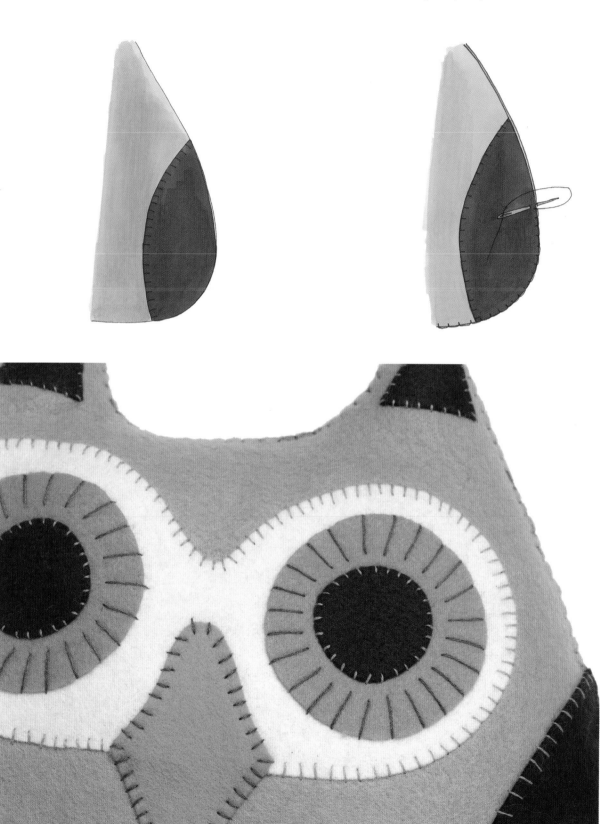

Sleepy Fox Pillow

What could be more peaceful than watching an animal sleeping? There is something so cosy and safe about it and I love the way many animals curl up in a ball. Foxes are beautiful animals and they seem to use their bushy tail as a blanket or pillow to get extra comfortable. When I saw a photograph of a sleepy fox, I knew I had to make one as a pillow. It looks great on a chair or a bed and looking at it is enough to make anyone want to curl up and go to sleep – perfect for a child's bedroom.

1 Cut out the templates and transfer to the felt. You will need two bodies and one head in the rusty brown, one tail and two ears in white and one nose in dark brown.

2 Split your thread to use only two or three strands (see page 10). Start by embroidering the eyes on the face with backstitch and long straight stitches for the eyelashes. You can use the dotted lines on the template as a guide and draw them with a faint pencil line on the felt.

4 Using the dotted line on the pattern as a guide, pin the white tail end in place on the front body and stitch in place with overhand or blanket stitch. Do not stitch the bottom edge yet. Embroider the line for the rest of the tail with backstitch.

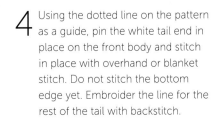

YOU WILL NEED

- Fox body, head, ear, nose and tail templates (page 123)

MATERIALS
- Rusty brown felt, at least 80 x 42cm (31½ x 16½in)
- Dark brown felt, 5 x 5cm (2 x 2in)
- White felt, 20 x 20cm (8 x 8in)
- Dark brown embroidery thread
- Toy stuffing, about 100g (3½oz)

TOOLS
- Scissors (paper, fabric and embroidery)
- Pen or pencil
- Pins
- Embroidery needle

3 Position the white ears on the face and stitch with overhand or blanket stitch using brown embroidery thread. Sew the brown nose on with a few small stitches.

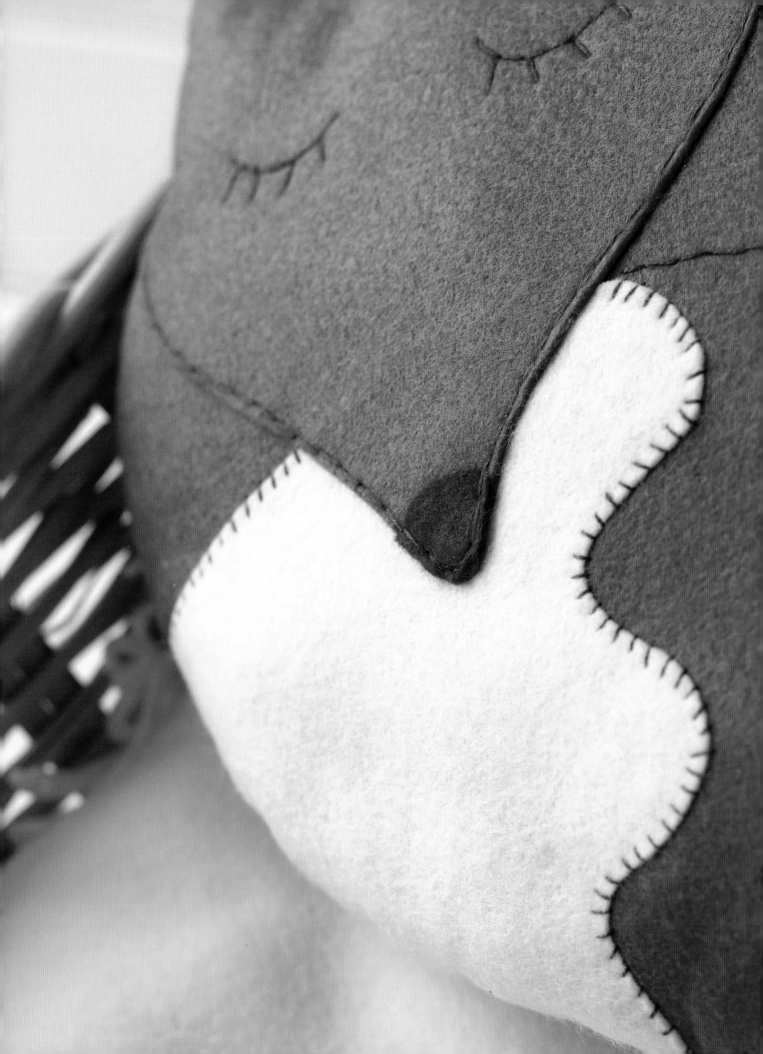

5 Place the head on the front body with the nose over the tail end. Secure in place with backstitch about 5mm (¼in) from the edge. Leave the top of the head unstitched.

6 Place the front body piece on top of the back piece and sew together with blanket stitch. Fill with the toy stuffing before closing completely. Make sure you are sewing all layers together when sewing the lower edge of the tail. You should be sewing though three layers then.

7 Find a comfortable spot for your new friend and he should be very happy with you.

Toy Bunny

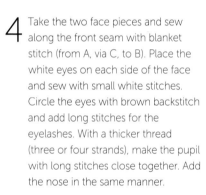

This cuddly bunny has a bit of a retro look about him and will look beautiful sitting on a chair or a bed. He would make a lovely gift for a child but do not use buttons if you are making it for a very small child. You could make him a whole selection of clothes.

YOU WILL NEED

- Bunny templates: body, leg, arm, head, face, shorts, eye and ear (page 128)

MATERIALS

- Beige felt for the body, at least 50 x 30cm (20 x 12in)

- Felt for the shorts, 16 x 14cm (6¼ x 5½in)

- Felt for the scarf, 40 x 3cm (16 x 1¼in)

- White felt, 13 x 13cm (5 x 5in)

- Dark brown, white, a colour to match the shoes and body embroidery thread

- Toy stuffing, about 80g (2¾oz)

- 4 small buttons

- Ribbon, 50cm (20in)

TOOLS

- Scissors (paper, fabric and embroidery)

- Pen or pencil

- Pins

- Embroidery needle

1 Cut out the templates and transfer to the felt. You will need two bodies, four legs, four arms, two faces and two ears in the body colour, two ears and two eyes in white and two shorts.

2 Snip into the ends of the scarf felt at regular intervals, about 1cm (½in) apart, 4cm (1½in) deep to make the fringes.

3 Split your thread to use only two strands (see page 10). Sew the white ears on top of the beige ones with blanket stitch all the way round. Make the arms and legs by sewing two pieces together in pairs with blanket stitch, and filling.

4 Take the two face pieces and sew along the front seam with blanket stitch (from A, via C, to B). Place the white eyes on each side of the face and sew with small white stitches. Circle the eyes with brown backstitch and add long stitches for the eyelashes. With a thicker thread (three or four strands), make the pupil with long stitches close together. Add the nose in the same manner.

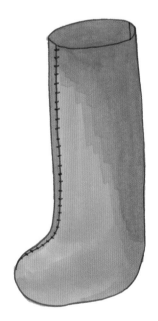

5 Close the seam from E to F on the head piece. Fold the base of the ears as shown and pin inside the face following the guide on the template. Add the head piece at the back so that the base of each ear is sandwiched between the face and the head. Sew all the way round with blanket stitch, from D to D, matching A to F at the top. Leave the neck open and fill the head.

6 Attach the front and back body pieces to the head with small overhand stitches. Insert the arms between the front and back body pieces, and sew each side with blanket stitch, going through the arms to hold firmly in place. Fill the body and insert the legs at the bottom (making sure the feet will be facing forward!). Close with blanket stitch going through the legs to hold.

7 Take both sides of the shorts and sew from A to B and to C on the other side with matching blanket stitch. Open the shorts so that the seams are in the middle and stitch from D to B and down to E for each leg. Place the shorts on your bunny. Cut the ribbon in half, sew one end with a button on top, on one side of the shorts (at the front) and cross over the shoulder at the back. Sew the other end with a ribbon on top, at the back. Trim the end if it is too long. Repeat on the other side. Tie the scarf around your bunny's neck.

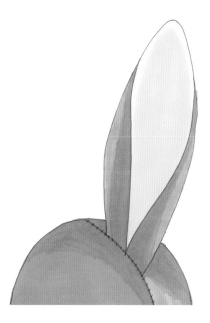

Wall Hanging Organiser

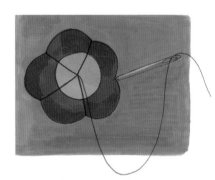

This lovely wall hanging will add a splash of colour on your wall in the kitchen, living room, bedroom or office. It is also practical because of the pocket which is large enough to hold letters, cards, invitations, receipts or vouchers. This would make a delightful gift for someone moving into a new home. You could personalise it with a name or a message of your choice.

YOU WILL NEED

- Pocket, house, roof, door, tree, trunk, flower, flower centre and leaf templates (page 124)

MATERIALS

- Light blue felt at least 36 x 62cm (14¼ x 24½in)
- Light green felt, 20 x 31cm (8 x 12¼in)
- Red felt, 10 x 15cm (4 x 6in)
- Felt for 4 houses, 6 x 4cm (2¼ x 1½in each)
- Felt for flowers, trees and doors in at least 4 colours including green and brown for trees, 10 x 10cm (4 x 4in) each
- Red, brown and green embroidery thread thread
- 40cm (16in) of ribbon

TOOLS

- Scissors (paper, fabric and embroidery)
- Pen or pencil
- Pins
- Embroidery needle

1 Cut out the templates and transfer to the felt. Cut your light blue felt in half to make two rectangles of 36 x 31cm (14¼ x 12¼in). Cut one green pocket, four houses, roofs and doors, three trees and trunks, eight flowers and flower centres and ten leaves. For all your embroidery I would advise splitting the thread and using only one strand.

2 Start by decorating the green pocket: make the stems of the flowers, as straight lines of about 4cm (1½in), with backstitch. You will need eight in total. Some can start from the bottom edge and some can be higher up. Attach the leaves at the base of the stems that are higher up with backstitch going through the middle. Place the flowers at the top of the stems and flower centres in the middle. Sew with a large star stitch going from the middle of the circle to the base of each petal. Finish the curved top edge of the pocket with blanket stitch.

3 Pin the pocket at the bottom of one of the blue rectangles. Following the curve of the pocket, pin the houses on. Add the tree trunks in between. Take the pocket off for now and sew the houses and tree trunks onto the blue felt with blanket stitch or small overhand stitches.

Add the roofs and the green tree shapes in the same manner. Embroider small straight lines as branches with backstitch and place a few French knots to look like blossoms or fruits. Sew the doors on all houses with backstitch and make square windows with straight stitches. If you wish to add a message or a name, trace it with a faint pencil line and embroider with backstitch.

4 Place the embroidered blue panel on top of the other one. Place one end of the ribbon between the two pieces of felt at the top, about 5–6cm (2–2¼in) from the right corner and do the same with the other end on the other side. Pin in place. Pin the pocket at the bottom and sew all the way round the panel with blanket stitch, making sure you sew though the three layers where the pocket is and through the ribbon to hold securely.

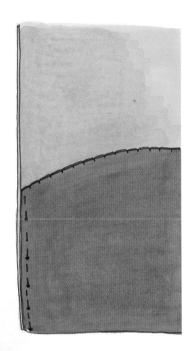

Hedgehog Pillow

This hedgehog pillow will bring the woodland into your home, but don't worry, there is nothing spiky about this cuddly friend. You could make a whole family of hedgehogs by reducing the pattern to make some smaller ones. This project will require a little bit of patience, as each spine needs blanket stitch around it but it is worth it. The finished project will look great. You could also have fun and make your hedgehog with some colourful spines by using different colours of felt.

YOU WILL NEED

- Hedgehog body, face, eye, nose and spine templates (page 118)

MATERIALS
- Dark brown felt at least 80 x 60cm (31½ x 23½in)
- Beige felt, 20 x 27cm (8 x 11in)
- Dark brown and bright turquoise embroidery thread
- Toy stuffing, about 100g (3½oz)

TOOLS
- Scissors (paper, fabric and embroidery)
- Pen or pencil
- Pins
- Embroidery needle

1 Cut out the templates and transfer to the felt. You will need two bodies, one nose, one eye and 65 spines in the brown felt and two faces in the beige felt.

2 Split your thread to use only two or three strands (see page 10). Start by placing the eye on the face and sew with small stitches. Add three or four eyelashes with long straight stitches. Do this for both face pieces.

3 Place the nose on the pointed bit of the face and sew with a few small stitches. The spines will need a blanket stitched edge with the turquoise thread (or another colour of your choice), at least on the sides. You can, if you wish, keep the base of the triangle unstitched as this will be hidden when layering the spines.

4 Lay the front body piece flat on your work surface and start placing the spines along the edge, in a line next to each other. Pin in place. Place another line of spines, overlapping the previous one slightly so that it hides the base of the first row and gives more volume. Pin in place. Keep doing this until you have reached the other edge. You now need to join the face to the body. Start with the front pieces (face with features and body with the spines pinned on it) and overlap them slightly, as shown. Use blanket stitch, making sure you are sewing through all three layers (the head, the body and the row of spines).

Repeat for the two back pieces (body and face – there are no spines this time).

5 Next you need to sew all the spines which are still pinned onto the body. Use a simple straight stitch as this will be hidden by the other layers and it is a good idea to use the brown thread to be even more discreet.

TIP: try to catch only the corner of the spines on the edges and then lift the spines out of the way as you carry on sewing.

6 When all the spines have been sewn onto the body, place the front onto the back and sew together with blanket stitch. Fill the hedgehog before closing it completely.

Children's Wall Hanging

When I was about five or six, we had a picture of a fawn made out of wire that used to fascinate me. I used to follow its lines with my finger and later draw its outline with a pencil. I must have made hundreds of drawings of this little fawn so that when I looked for inspiration for a wall hanging for children, I knew it had to be my little fawn! Here he is in true retro style.

1 Cut out the templates and transfer to the felt. You will need to cut two blue frames, one white inner frame, one green tree and one brown trunk and fawn. For all your embroidery, split the thread and use only one strand.

2 Start by pinning the fawn and the tree foliage onto the white inner frame. Sew in place with small overhand stitches. Make a few branches with backstitches and cherries with French knots on the tree. Sew on the trunk with small stitches too and add a few cherries on the ground (with French knots). Add a few strands of grass with backstitches. Make some white spots on the back of the fawn with French knots and embroider his eye as a curve (backstitch) plus eyelashes (long straight stitches).

3 Pin the white inner frame onto one blue frame (centre it) and sew with small discreet white stitches all the way round.

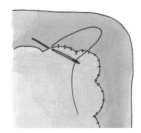

4 Place the pompom trim all the way round the plain blue frame and add the other blue frame (with the appliqué picture) on top, so that the braid part of the pompom trim is sandwiched between the two pieces of blue felt and the pompoms are sticking out. Trim the end as required to make a perfect, unbroken border. Add the ribbon loop by placing each end between the two pieces of felt, about 4cm (1½in) from each corner at the top.

Sew all the way round with blanket stitch, making sure you go through both pieces of felt and the pompom trim as well as the ribbon ends.

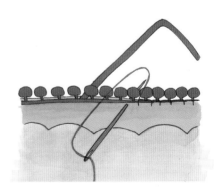

YOU WILL NEED

- Frame, inner frame, tree, trunk and fawn templates (page 127)

MATERIALS
- Light blue felt, at least 35 x 20cm (13¾ x 8in)
- White felt, 15 x 19cm (6 x 7½in)
- Green felt, 5 x 8cm (2 x 3¼in)
- Dark brown felt, 10 x 11cm (4 x 4¼in)
- Red, brown, white and green embroidery thread
- 20cm (8in) of red ribbon (for the hanging loop)
- 120cm (47¼in) of small red pompom trim

TOOLS
- Scissors (paper, fabric and embroidery)
- Pen or pencil
- Pins
- Embroidery needle

Templates

CHRISTMAS LAVENDER BAG

——————————	Long stitch
— — — — — —	Back stitch
▬ ▬ ▬ ▬ ▬ ▬	Mock feather stitch
· · · · · · · · · · · ·	Chain stitch (Lazy-daisy stitch)
- - - - - - - - - -	French knots

HEART HANGING

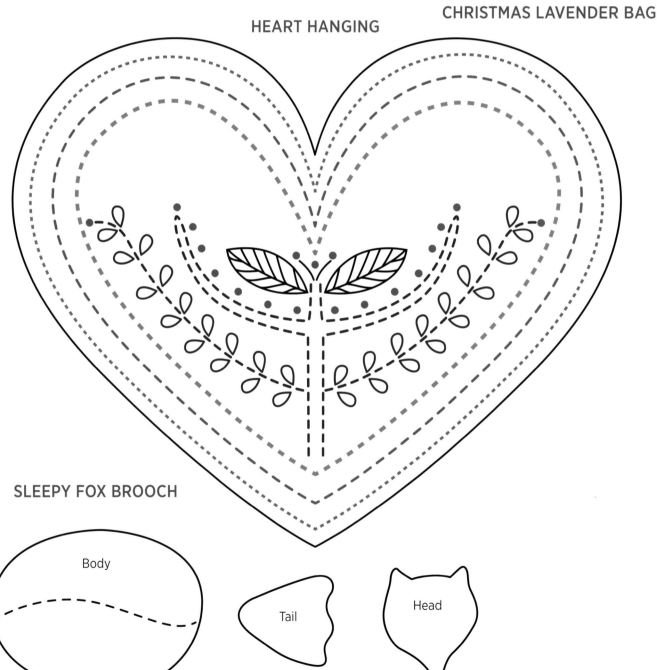

SLEEPY FOX BROOCH

Body

Tail

Head

116

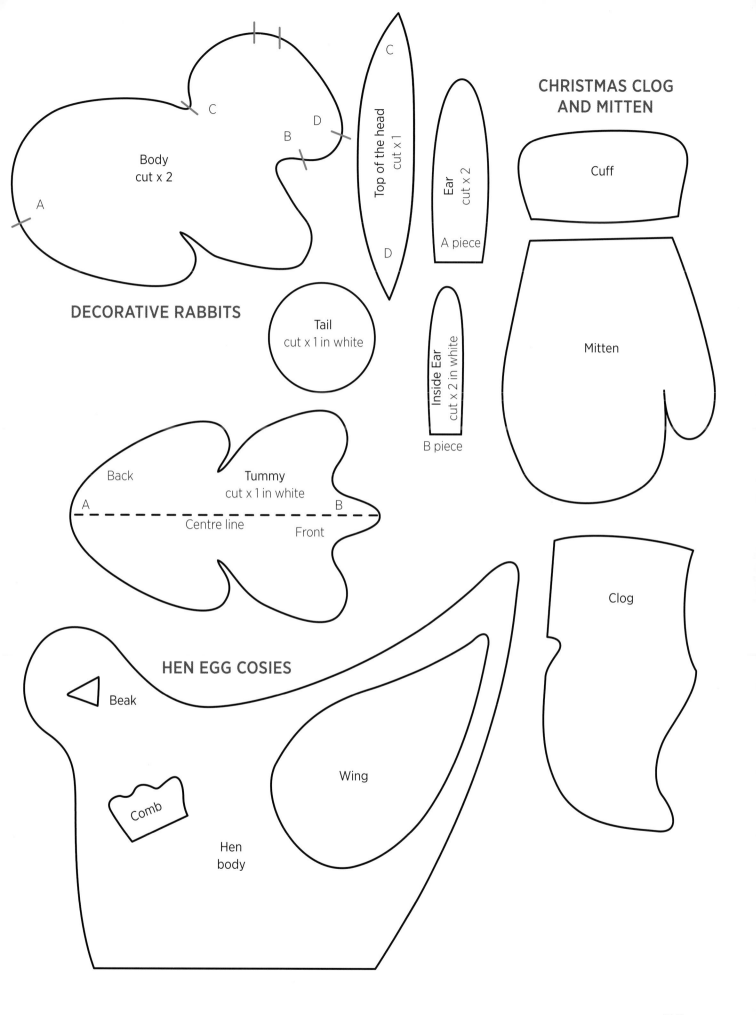

Body
cut x 2

C

C
D
B

A

DECORATIVE RABBITS

Top of the head
cut x 1

C

D

Ear
cut x 2

A piece

CHRISTMAS CLOG
AND MITTEN

Cuff

Tail
cut x 1 in white

Inside Ear
cut x 2 in white

B piece

Mitten

Back

Tummy
cut x 1 in white

A

Centre line

Front

B

Clog

HEN EGG COSIES

Beak

Wing

Comb

Hen
body

117

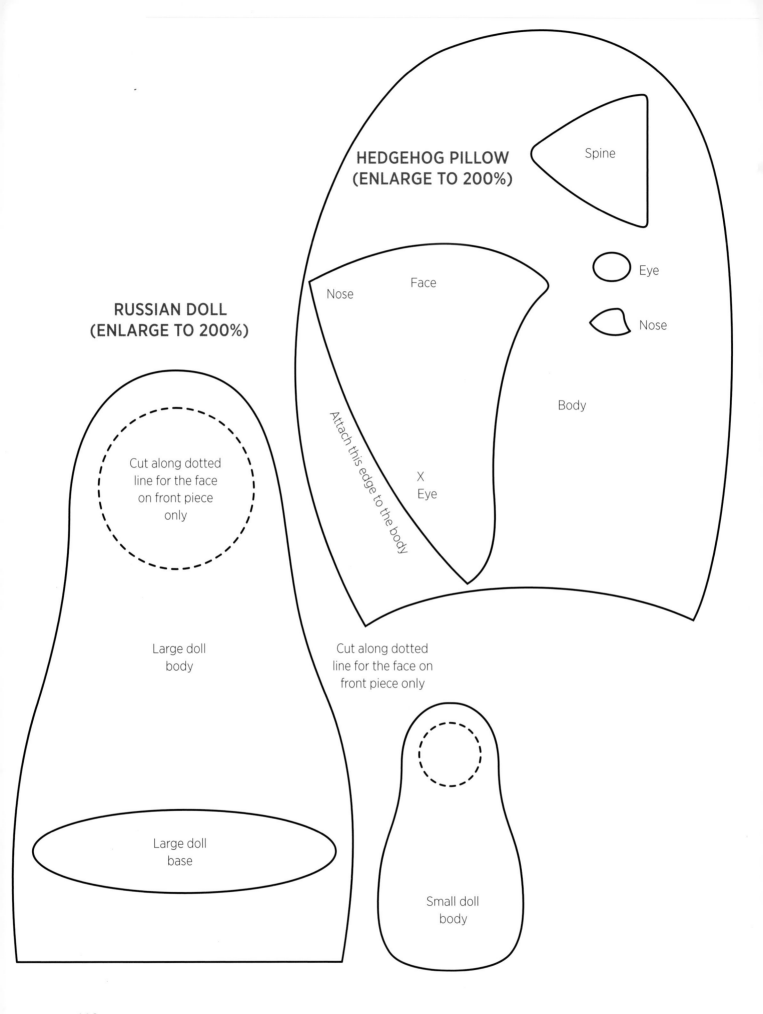

**HEDGEHOG PILLOW
(ENLARGE TO 200%)**

Spine

Face

Nose

Eye

Nose

Body

Attach this edge to the body

X
Eye

Cut along dotted
line for the face on
front piece only

**RUSSIAN DOLL
(ENLARGE TO 200%)**

Cut along dotted
line for the face
on front piece
only

Large doll
body

Large doll
base

Small doll
body

SCANDI HORSE

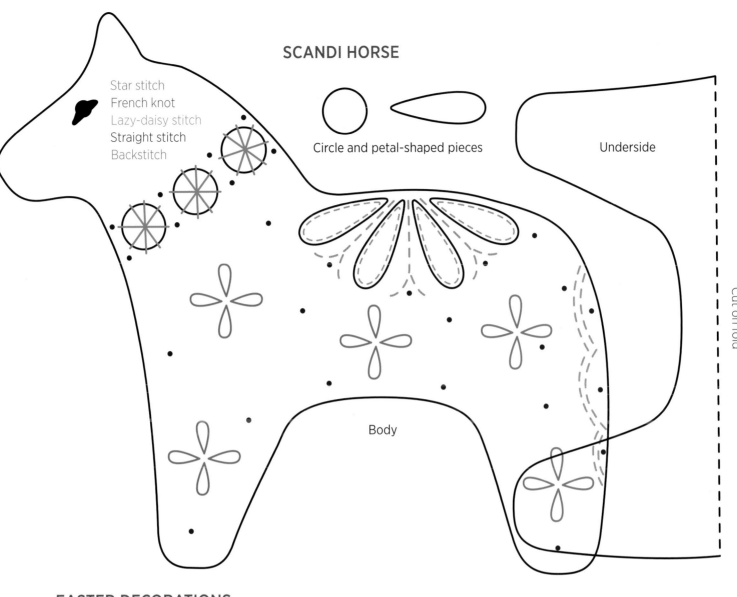

Star stitch
French knot
Lazy-daisy stitch
Straight stitch
Backstitch

Circle and petal-shaped pieces

Underside

Cut on fold

Body

EASTER DECORATIONS

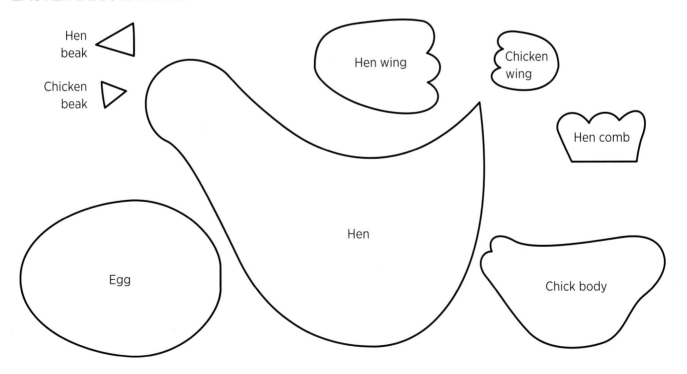

Hen beak

Chicken beak

Hen wing

Chicken wing

Hen comb

Hen

Egg

Chick body

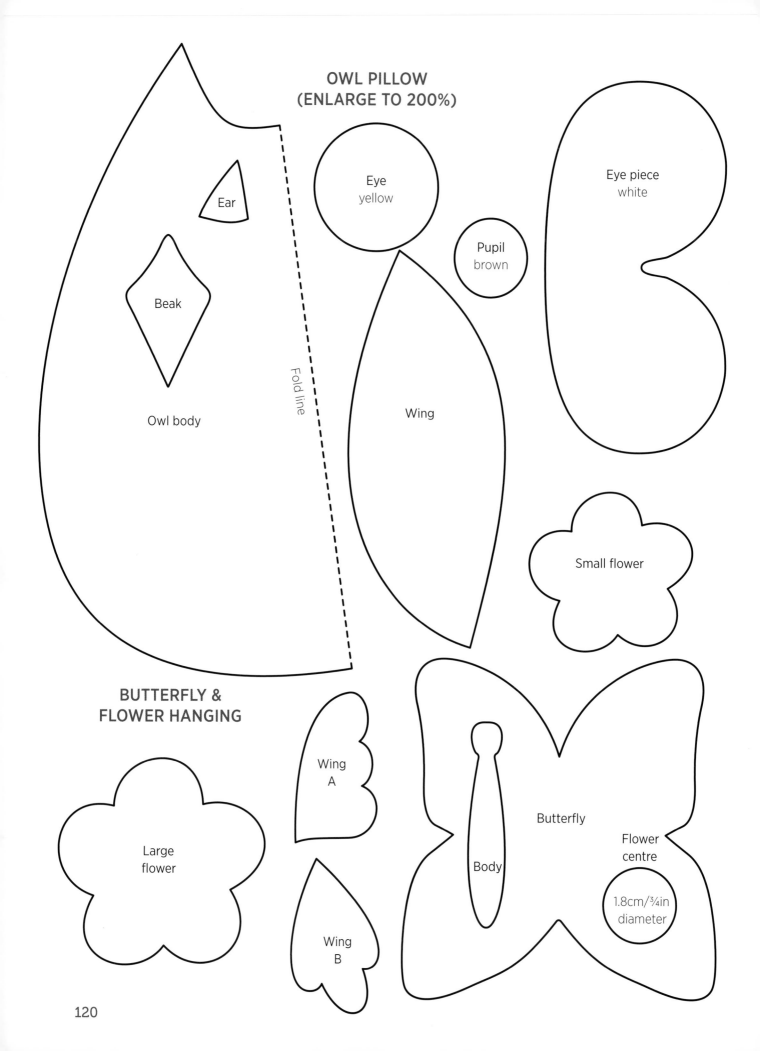

OWL PILLOW
(ENLARGE TO 200%)

Ear

Eye
yellow

Pupil
brown

Eye piece
white

Beak

Fold line

Owl body

Wing

Small flower

BUTTERFLY &
FLOWER HANGING

Wing
A

Large
flower

Body

Butterfly

Flower
centre

1.8cm/¾in
diameter

Wing
B

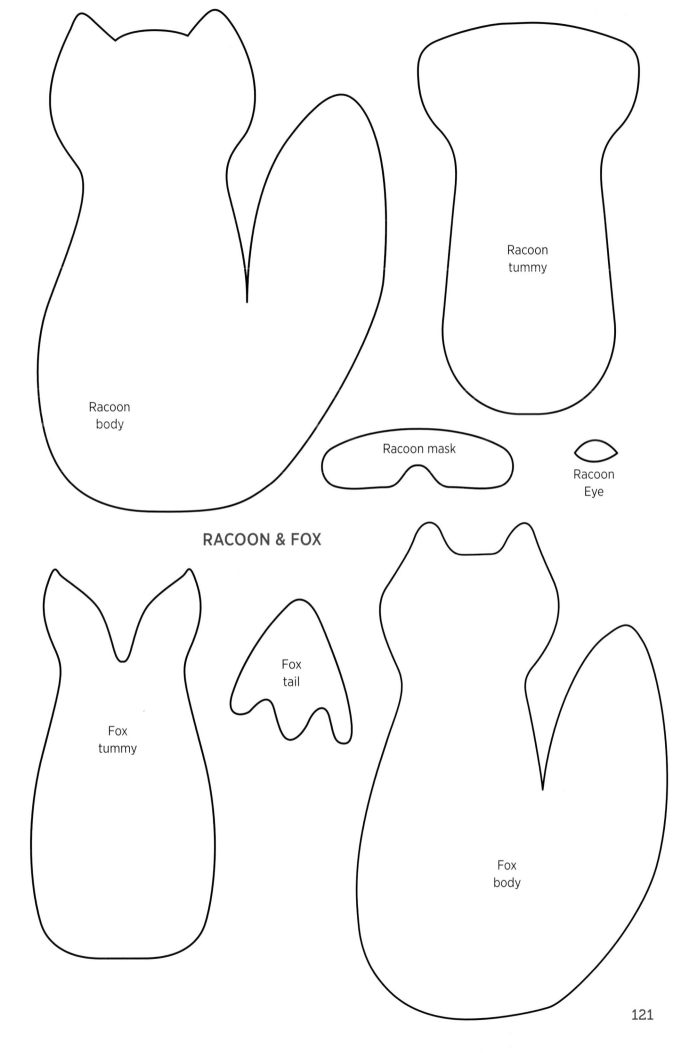

Racoon tummy

Racoon body

Racoon mask

Racoon Eye

RACOON & FOX

Fox tummy

Fox tail

Fox body

121

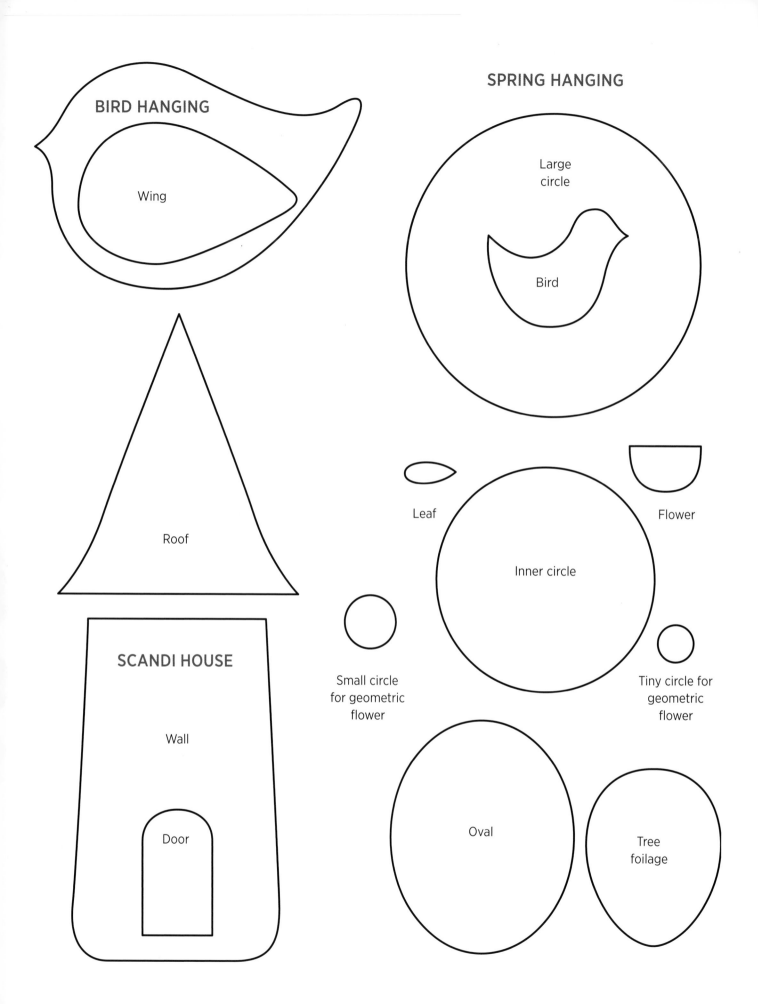

BIRD HANGING

Wing

SPRING HANGING

Large circle

Bird

Roof

Leaf

Flower

Inner circle

SCANDI HOUSE

Small circle for geometric flower

Tiny circle for geometric flower

Wall

Door

Oval

Tree foilage

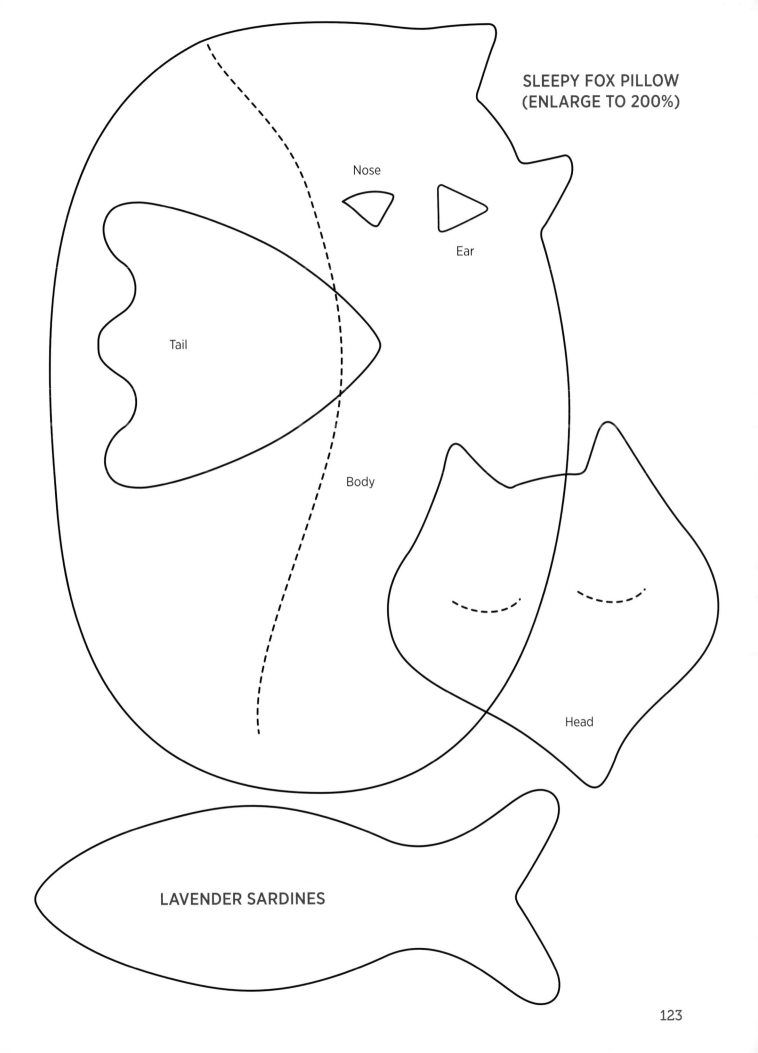

SLEEPY FOX PILLOW
(ENLARGE TO 200%)

Nose

Ear

Tail

Body

Head

LAVENDER SARDINES

123

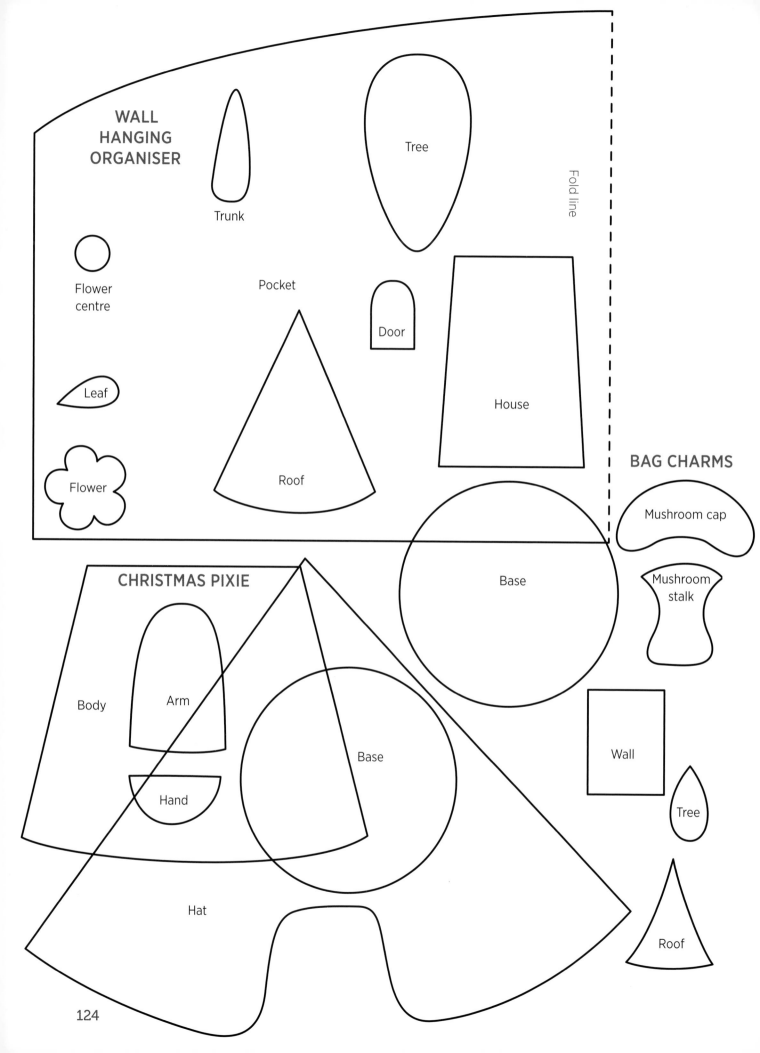

WALL
HANGING
ORGANISER

Trunk

Tree

Fold line

Flower centre

Pocket

Door

House

Leaf

Roof

BAG CHARMS

Flower

Mushroom cap

Base

Mushroom stalk

CHRISTMAS PIXIE

Body

Arm

Base

Hand

Wall

Base

Tree

Hat

Roof

124

MUG COSY

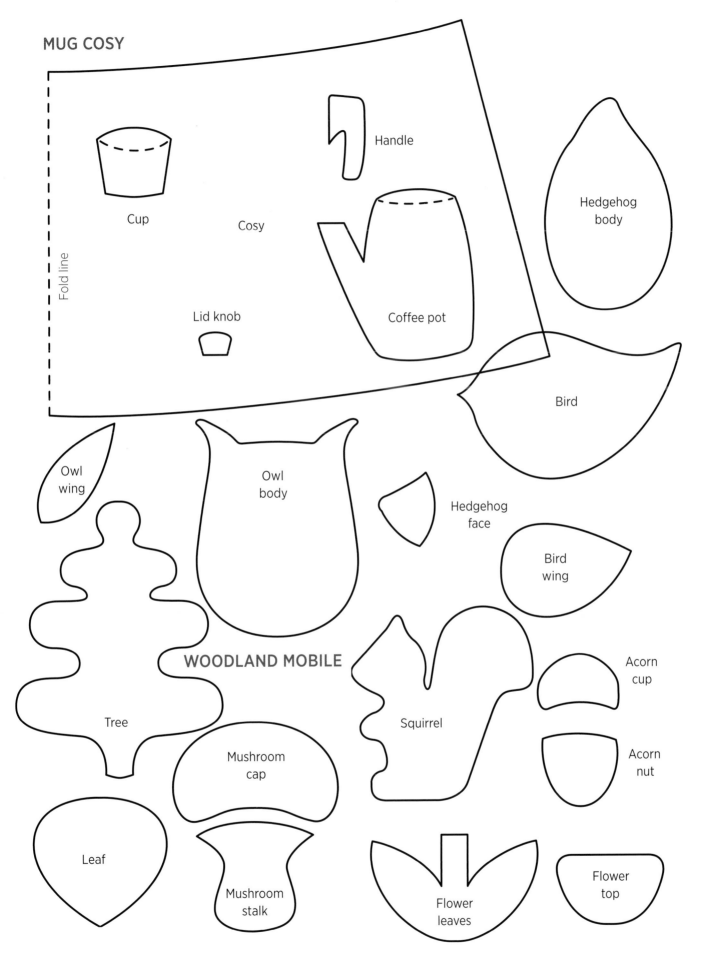

Handle

Cup

Cosy

Fold line

Lid knob

Coffee pot

Hedgehog body

Bird

Owl wing

Owl body

Hedgehog face

Bird wing

WOODLAND MOBILE

Tree

Squirrel

Acorn cup

Acorn nut

Mushroom cap

Leaf

Mushroom stalk

Flower leaves

Flower top

HALLOWEEN DECORATIONS

Cut curve on
front piece only

Dress

Bloomers

Cat
face

Shoe

Cat

Hat

Stockings

FLOWER BROOCHES

Base

Flower

ROSE BROOCHES

Circle
4cm (1½in) diameter

Roof

BEACH HUT BUNTING

Window

Hut

Bunting

SCANDI-STYLE PILLOW

Large oblong

Small oblong

Teardrop shape

Large triangle

Small circle

Leaf

Small triangle

Medium circle

Large circle

Tree trunk

Fawn

Fold line

CHILDREN'S WALL HANGING

Frame

Inner frame

Tree foilage

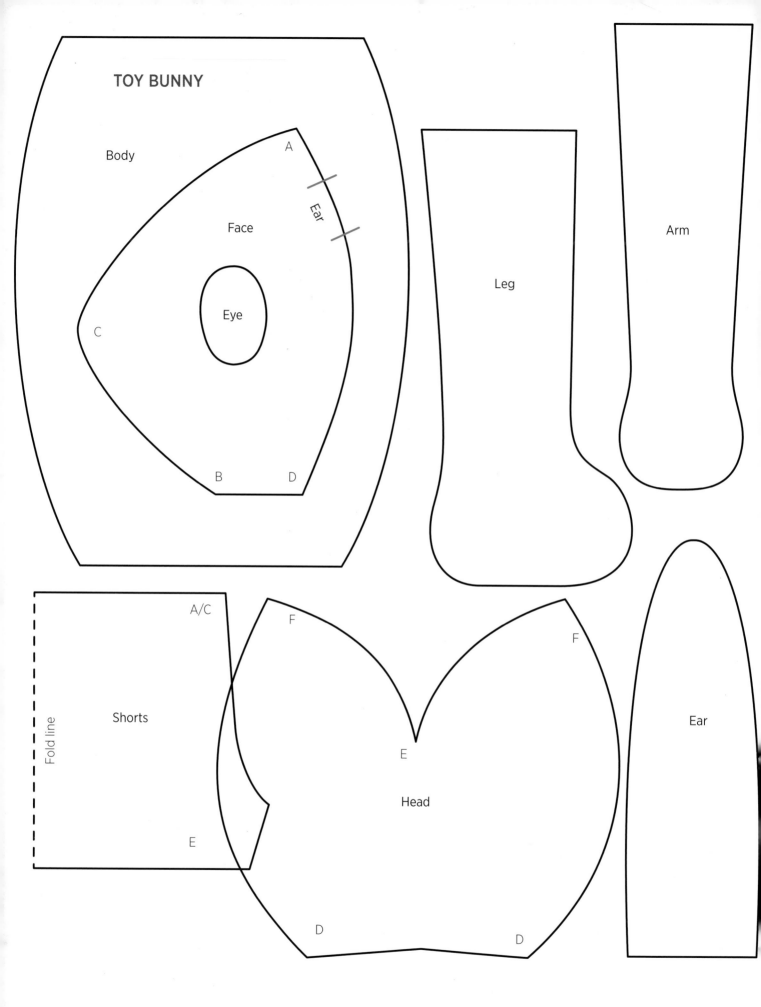

TOY BUNNY

Body

Face

Ear

Eye

A

C

B

D

Leg

Arm

A/C

Fold line

Shorts

E

F

F

E

Head

Ear

D

D

128